3—

CFW

Collective Fashion Wisdom
90 Questions / 450 Answers / 5 Points of View

by Joyce Elkus & Nancy Brinker
with Jay Ott, Liz Ricketts and Craig Signer
Illustrated by Margaret Voelker-Ferrier

For further information, contact the publisher at:

Keen Custom Media
306 Greenup St.
Covington, KY 41011

ISBN 978-0-9647083-7-2

Printed in Canada
First edition, first printing

Editor: Stephanie Sung
Designer: Jesse Reed

COLLECTIVE FASHION WISDOM

90 Questions / 450 Answers / 5 Points of View

by Joyce Elkus & Nancy Brinker
with Jay Ott, Liz Ricketts, and Craig Signer

Illustrated by Margaret Voelker-Ferrier

Contents

For all those who love fashion (*but wish it were easier to get dressed*)!

You know style when you see it—but how do you get it? We all know that shopping alone won't make you stylish, but this book helps you figure out how to dress not just for success, but for elegance, style, and grace. These five experts answer all your questions about clothes, fashion, and much else. Their witty, insightful, and easy-to-understand answers to basic questions we all face when we figure out how to greet the world will help us all become more stylish. We should be grateful to Joyce Elkus and Nancy Brinker for providing us with this compendium of fashion wisdom and bon mots.

Aaron Betsky
Director, Cincinnati Art Museum

After retiring from Saks Fifth Avenue in 2007, people continued to ask me questions related to fashion. The thought occurred to me that perhaps I could answer some of these questions in book form and I immediately reached out to Nancy Brinker. Nancy was formerly the Fashion and Public Relations Director at Saks Fifth Avenue, and I had always admired her presentations, the quality of her work, and her fashion savvy. We met and discussed the possibility of writing the book together, and although we both have busy lives, we knew we wanted to do the project.

We decided to use the FAQ format for our book, meaning we would compile commonly asked "fashion" questions and answer them individually. I was appointed point person and was to set the assignments and deadlines. Eventually we added more contributors: Jay Ott, designer; Liz Ricketts, stylist; Craig Signer, designer for Craig Signer Designs; and Margaret Voelker-Ferrier, illustrator.

What formed was a book depicting five different viewpoints. Each of the contributors has a distinct style and something unique to teach budding fashionistas but what links us is that fashion has played a central role in all of our lives.

Joyce Elkus

In a highly visual world, the way we look speaks louder and to a larger audience than the words we say. Some people choose not to emphasize appearance. Others simply don't think they have the skill to put themselves together. Joyce convinced me that this might be the audience for another fashion book, and my admiration for her compelled me to sign on for the project. It was of utmost importance for me to present several points of view in our book. Style is so highly personal that there are no simple rules… no universal answers. You may identify more strongly with one contributor than the other. We hope the fact that we often disagree gives you comfort and confidence in the truth that when it comes to personal style, there is no right and no wrong.

Nancy Brinker

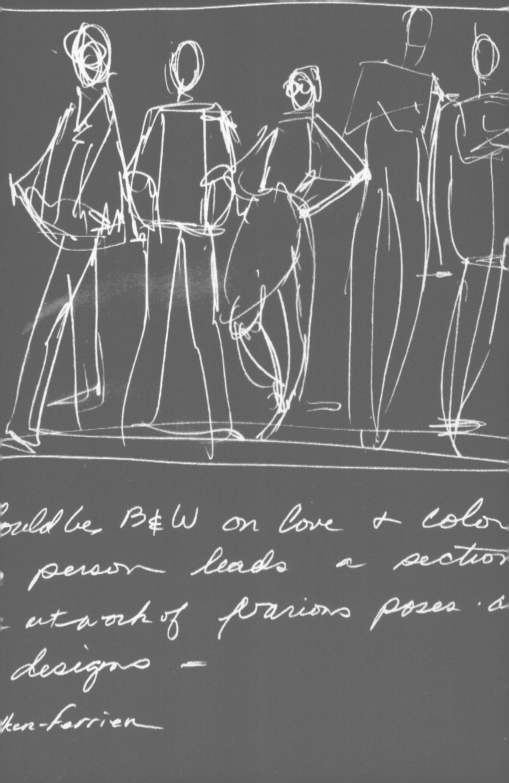

could be B&W or one + color
person leads a section
art work of various poses
designs -

ken-ferrien

Contributors

Joyce

—

Model, Buyer, Personal Shopper
Elegant & Classic

Fashion has always been an important part of my life. In fact, my mother often said that even at age two, I insisted on matching all my hair bows with my socks. I only wanted to wear skirts, too. As a preteen, I was always given the choice of a birthday party or a shopping trip to the Saks Fifth Avenue in Detroit. I invariably would choose the shopping trip. When the day arrived, I sat in anticipation for the 45 minute drive from my hometown of Toledo, Ohio to the store. Upon arrival, I darted excitedly from one display to another, and flitted from department to department. I scanned the merchandise with great speed, trying to see everything at once. My mother certainly had a hard time keeping up with me. I have such wonderful memories of these trips.

When I learned to drive, my trips to Detroit became more frequent. My mother let me select all of her clothes as well as my own, and she always loved my choices. I cannot remember that she ever returned a single item I selected. Looking back, I imagine this is where the confidence in my fashion sense first developed. In high school and college I began modeling, which furthered my romance with the fashion world. After an unexpected divorce, I went to work as the Designer Buyer for a specialty store in Cincinnati, Ohio. I learned so much about the industry as well as how to deal with the public. I truly loved going to all the major fashion shows—Blass, Beene, Oscar, Trigere, Halston, Adolfo, Scassi and many others. Unfortunately, within two years, the owner experienced severe financial reverses and I left the position. I was soon hired as the Director of the Fifth Avenue Club at Saks Fifth Avenue in Cincinnati. The Fifth Avenue Club was the executive shopping service for Saks Fifth Avenue, and here I became involved in organizing trunk shows and special Club events, marketing, managing, and community involvement. I maintained this very interesting job for 22 years.

I received my B.A. from the University of Cincinnati, and taught second grade for 3 years. I have two sons, Marc and Jason Greenberg. Both live in New York City. I also have two wonderful grandchildren, Zac and Hannah Greenberg.

Nancy
—

Buyer, Fashion Director, Fashion Educator
Minimalist Clothing/Excessive Accessories

A few dim childhood memories of mine include a blue dress with "diamonds," a green vinyl handbag full of discarded costume jewelry, and hours spent playing with jewelry boxes. This early attraction formed the basis of my lifelong style. My cousin, Karen, was my original inspiration. She was a buyer, and I was attracted to her lifestyle, her spirit, and her look. I followed her lead, becoming a buyer for the H&S Pogue Company in Cincinnati, Ohio. Subsequent positions as the Corporate Wardrobe Consultant for the regional Casual Corner stores and later for Saks Fifth Avenue introduced me to many women in search of style. A key responsibility in these roles was to speak to groups on the "art of dressing." I've spoken to thousands of women about the topic. I have a strong sense of the issues around clothing and style, and empathize with those who struggle to get dressed. In 1988, I became the Fashion and Special Events Director for SFA Cincinnati. For 10 years, I oversaw the details of the store's fashion and community events, and enjoyed constant exposure to beautiful clothing and the women (and men) who love it.

I have taught as an adjunct instructor in the fashion program at the University of Cincinnati College of Design, Architecture, Art, and Planning for 12 years and am currently the Assistant Director of the College's School of Design. Young graphic, digital, industrial, and fashion designers provide joy and inspiration. My M.A. in Art History from UC's School of Art focused on the making of fame through the mechanics of networking, publicity, and appearance. I have concluded my course-work toward a Ph.D. in Art History focusing on the intersections between art and fashion.

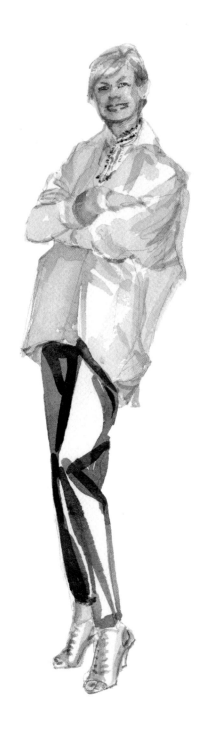

Jay

—

Designer
Provocative Purist

I live in New York where I am the designer of a luxury men's and women's apparel line. I studied fashion design at The University of Cincinnati. While still in College, I apprenticed with Ralph Rucci, John Bartlett, Coach, Stan Herman, Liz Claiborne, and had my own small line which I sold at local Cincinnati retailer Suki (sadly now out of business). I was one of those lucky kids who knew at a young age what I wanted to do. My mom recalls me saying at age 3 that I wanted to be Ralph Lauren.

I used to go shopping all the time with my mom, and I was obsessed with fashion television, videos, and Fashion File when I was in elementary school. I made my first dress out of garbage bags and staples in 7th grade, and I continued down this path (eventually introducing a glue gun) until I got my first sewing machine in my junior year of high school. Then, everything changed.

I got a part-time job at the fabric store and sought the knowledge of my fellow employees who were amazing at-home sewers and craftsmen in their own rights. I have always been drawn to fabric and form and pursued my love of these elements in my designs. I truly don't remember a time when I wasn't into fashion. Some of my favorite designers are Geoffrey Beene, George Stavropoulos, Yohji Yamamoto, Ralph Rucci, Donna Karan, Christian Lacroix, Zack Carr, Norman Norell, Halston, and I could go on and on. I just believe in letting clothes live their lives and letting the wearer really use their clothing as they personally see fit. I like people first and design second. Nothing is more exciting than seeing the perfect person first and noticing the clothes right after. Too often, I see people whose identity is lost behind clothing.

I was born in Toledo, Ohio and moved around a lot. I always wanted to move to New York. Now that I'm here, every year I feel more myself than ever before.

Liz

—

Designer, Stylist
"Idea Fairy"

I would never have guessed that I'd be involved in a project like this until this very moment. I have always felt that fashion was important but struggled to accept that I valued it. I grew up in a small town near Flint, Michigan—not exactly a fashion hub. And yet, somehow, my mother made me aware of fashion. I don't recall her telling me what was "in style" and she was never fooled by my "need" for this or that designer piece. She simply approached fashion as an aesthetic and taught me to view the world through a lens of beauty. In Flint, clothes indicated status and style was defined by labels. It wasn't until design school that I became aware of a different type of style. Everything from preppy to boho chic was accepted. I began to see fashion as an expression of identity. I chose to work in NYC for most of my internship quarters in design, retail, and styling. My concept of style continued to evolve. I met people who I was unable to categorize and realized that I didn't need or want to put them into a style category. It was inspiring to appreciate someone's individual style and realize that even if I had the same hair, body, and clothing, I wouldn't look the same. After NYC, I became my own style concept. I spent part of 2009 working in London, where my ideas of beauty and style converged. I was fortunate to be surrounded by people who cared about fashion as a means to add beauty to their lives. To them, style was not about being unique, but rather about feeling beautiful. Concepts of beauty were further realized through fashion. Choosing beauty seemed to be a community concern, and they affirmed my mother's message that choosing beauty is important.

Are those who dismiss fashion suggesting that aesthetics are not important? A beautiful mind can manifest outwardly. It is not a question of why fashion should matter but of why we might not want it to matter. Being aware of beauty in this highly personal aspect of our lives can increase our desire to seek and choose the most beautiful options in other areas. Fashion offers us the chance to control how we see the world.

Craig

—

Designer
Textile Specialist

Like most top models never went to modeling schools and most famous artists never went to art school, I never attended a design school. I didn't spend my childhood daydreaming about someday being discovered, however invariably, as if almost by magic someone appears out of the woodwork and they get discovered. Ironically enough, I began my career by turning down a scholarship to Pratt Institute in New York which I won while at Miami Beach High School. Instead, I moved to the West Coast and took a job designing advertisements. A year later, I enrolled at UCLA for business and marketing, which led to an immediate career in global product design, complete with first class travel all over the world.

My turning point occurred in Paris where I worked for a textile mill. It seems I was a master at choosing the right yarns and perfect colors used to design couture fabrics. The late Cecile Rothschild, whose family lineage comes as close to royalty as you can get, heard about me and invited me to her apartment (the former Coco Chanel residence). We became friends. Although she was Karl Lagerfeld's biggest couture client, she encouraged me to begin a career in fashion design. I never even imagined my becoming a fashion designer, but Madame Rothschild did. I credit her for discovering me. Today, my fashion company is devoted to producing impeccable hand-finished garments with customized details, and precision cuts for both men and women. Red carpet style gowns and over-the-top high waist pants are a few of my signature styles.

I was born in Cincinnati, but now reside in Florida where my design studio overlooks both Miami Beach and downtown Miami. The Craig Signer Collection is sold at Saks Fifth Avenue's Fifth Avenue Clubs and other retail stores across the country.

Margaret

—

Illustrator

A fashion illustrator and designer who began her professional career in Paris working for G.A.P., a Trend Forecasting magazine for the fashion industry, Margaret made her reputation as one of the most important fashion insiders in Paris by also adding design and illustrations for Louis Feraud, Lanvin, Patou, as well as several other design houses and magazines to her résumé. After four years, she returned to the states and began a career as a professor of fashion design and illustration. She later received a Master's Degree in Arts Administration from the University of Cincinnati's CCM. In her various roles as Chairman, Coordinator, and Professor in the University of Cincinnati's Fashion Design Program, she has set about her goal of making the program recognized as one of the finest in the world. Margaret continues striving to increase its excellence with every opportunity, and her own illustrations, paintings, and watercolors have become increasingly collectible.

Style

"Fashion fades, style is eternal."
—Coco Chanel

1 — *What is style?*

Joyce

By birth or choice and very personal.

I believe a person can be born with natural style. Style can be created or it can be developed. Style is the way a person portrays his or herself in appearance to others. How one projects their inner self with clothing, accessories, body type and even posture are all a part of the total picture of style. There is no right or wrong "style." Style is very personal.

Nancy

Essence.

A number of years ago, I traveled to Italy intent on studying Italian fashion. Instead, I looked at Italian women. When I returned, I had no sense of the clothing they wore or the way they wore their hair. I had a sense of their style—something that had much more to do with a core or an essence. Style extends to posture, expression, humor, civility, passion. Style cannot be disassociated from fashion, but I believe it has more to do with presence, confidence and projection.

Jay

Learning, discovery, expression.

Style is a yearning to discover new experiences, objects, and passions and to be able to filter/express them in a way that is unique to you.

Liz

An internal presence made external.

Lord Chesterfield said, "Style is the dress of thoughts." Style is evidence of personal essence. It is fashion without trend and yes, without rules. Having style means you have discovered your own perspective and how to communicate it. Strong style provokes us to think beyond fashion and accept unique expression. When saying someone is stylish, we are recognizing individual beauty. To have style requires listening to your own thoughts and learning how to interpret them through your appearance. The result will be that other people view you as you view yourself.

Craig

Your look.

You are the definition of "a" style. Your style is defined by what you wear, where you wear it, how you wear it, and why you wear it. It is your outward and unspoken statement of how you would like others to see you socially.

2

Is style something that can be taught?

Joyce

Yes.

There are ways to help someone develop personal style. I have a classic style. Once, a customer's boyfriend wanted me to teach her about style. She was willing to learn and wanted to know how to develop a classic look. We worked together for about a year. Originally, she came to me with a pair of wooden clogs in a brown paper bag. By the end of the year, she understood fabric, design, and when and where to wear appropriate clothing. She had developed "style." I was very proud of her.

Nancy

Did Professor Higgins teach Eliza Doolittle?

Or, did he encourage a certain confidence by discovering a "diamond in the rough?" Diana Vreeland said: "Of course, one is born with good taste. It's very hard to acquire. You can acquire the *patina* of taste." You can show someone how to polish the exterior, but style comes from an interior place.

Jay

Style is non-specific.

What one might consider stylish, another might consider garish, tacky, or boring. Style grows proportionately to exposure. The more you see, the more you can cultivate an idea of who you are, what you love, and what you want to look like. Style doesn't come from teaching or lessons, but through awareness and self-reflection.

Liz

A connection to the sensory world.

Style is often called the "it" factor, implying you either have it or you don't. Some people are better at expressing themselves externally because they innately understand how to connect their thoughts and feelings with the rest of the sensory world. You have to trust yourself. I learned that my spontaneous decisions define my style and I have grown more comfortable listening to my instincts, whether it is to undo a button or add a ring. Spontaneity can't be taught because it has no rules. It can, however, be encouraged.

Craig

Principles applied with flair.

The principles of style can be taught, but someone must have flair to build, maintain and change styles.

3

What steps should I take to find my own personal style?

Joyce

Analyze. Study. Consult.

First, you should take a moment to analyze your life style. Do you work? Are you a stay at home mother? What types of clothing do you like? Then, think about people whom you admire either in your personal life, professional life, or even celebrities. Why do you like what they wear? Look through fashion magazines and fashion dailies like *WWD (Women's Wear Daily)*. Finally, seek advice from a personal consultant at a store. Little by little, you will develop your own style.

Nancy

A heightened awareness of personal aesthetic.

Keep looking and develop an awareness of what you find to be beautiful. Rip out pages of magazines with looks you relate or aspire to. Keep folders by color, occasion, silhouette. Most importantly, heighten your sensitivity to your own sense of comfort. Uncomfortable people don't exude style.

Jay

Know yourself.

First, turn off your TV. Next, stop looking at celebrities—let Nicole Kidman be Nicole Kidman! Next, open a book, any book—fiction, art, architecture, poetry, cooking. Next, find other people who have a desire for life and include them in your discoveries. Next, share your findings often and listen to those who share with you. Lastly, lose insecurities by surrounding yourself with honest people and honest things.

Liz

Put some thought into dressing.

Although I have learned to take it as a compliment, it confuses me when people look at me and say, "I could never wear that." I'm not sure why they picture themselves in my clothes. People often think that what they wear is different from other forms of self-expression. They might think carefully about what to say, but believe that thinking carefully about clothing is superfluous. Dressing requires self-analysis. What do you like? How do you feel most comfortable? Believe in your instincts. If you think something is ugly, then it is. If you think it is beautiful, then it is. Just because something may be in *Vogue* doesn't mean it's right for you.

"If you don't feel connected to your clothes, you won't have style."

Observing others whose style you relate to is fine if you have a sense of your own preferences and comfort level. Pay attention to your responses to the way other people look. What makes you look twice? What pieces provoke a feeling inside you? Keeping a file of images increases your awareness and can really inspire you. As you become more aware of what you like both in your own closet and outside of it you can begin to intelligently acquire new pieces. Remember that your style is the way you communicate non-verbally within your world. Clothing expresses the way you think about yourself. If you don't feel connected to your clothes, you won't have style. A good indication that you have discovered your own style is when everything in your closet appeals to you.

Craig

Ask yourself basic questions.

First, you should define your likes and dislikes in all social aspects. What do you do? Where do you go? Who are you with and what is your role? Secondly, define what you need. Then you can start buying wardrobe pieces that reflect your personal style.

Why is style important?

Joyce

Focus and self-expression.

Everyone needs to wear clothing. By developing a style, you can focus so much better when purchasing clothing and make wiser decisions. Style makes a statement about you to others. It is probably most important in the professional world.

Nancy

Display of confidence.

Style is important because it comes from self awareness. I love the thought of being comfortable in your own skin. An awareness of and an adherence to your personal style will improve and simplify your life. You will communicate well without speaking and avoid costly wardrobe mistakes.

Jay

Enhancement of personal value.

Style absolutely adds to the value of life and enhances the way we all live. If people tried to be the best version of themselves, they would be happier. No one wants to look at a sad, frumpy, insecure, uniformed anything.

Liz

An added voice.

Style is expressing your perspective through fashion.

Craig

An individual choice based on one's place in the world.

Important or not, everyone has his/her own style. It is non-verbal communication in the world in which you live. You choose how important your image and styles are in defining your role in society.

Should I stick to one genre of clothing or can I have a little

Joyce

Build on basics.

By and large, I like interchangeable pieces. It is nice to have exciting pieces that add punch too. Be wise when you purchase. Basic pieces should be the investment items. Fashion or trendy items are fun to add on a seasonal basis at a lesser price-point.

Nancy

Deliver a clear message.

I believe that persons of style have a consistency about their appearance. Buying all colors, all silhouettes, and all trends results in confusion and waste. I once worked with a person who rotated looks, moving from vamp to executive to little girl within days. I didn't know who I was dealing with. Being consistent with style isn't boring. There is a range of interpretations with a singular message.

Jay

The world is your playground.

You can have whatever you want. As you begin to see the big picture, you will find bits of things that don't look like "you," but once you put them on, place them in a room, read them on a page, you feel transformed. It goes back to knowing yourself but keeping an open mind.

bit of everything?

Life is the occasion.

Liz
Fashion rules are made to encourage creative ways of breaking them. You can create a place and time to wear anything.

Mix it up.

Craig
Always dress according to your lifestyle, but don't be afraid to explore beyond your comfort zone. It's great to mix advanced with classics and break suits up to be more individual. Break out and think of mixing something new and trendy with something classic you're holding onto already in your closet. Even Sharon Stone made fashion history by wearing a Gap t-shirt with a long skirt to the Emmy's and looked fabulous. I had her stylist, who loved a pair of our evening pants, only to want to take scissors to the hem of the beaded lace, rag the hemline, and pair it back to a tank top. Mix it up—it can be great.

6

Are there some people who can get away with breaking all rules?

Joyce

There are some people who never even think about "style."

They have their own unique style, and the confidence to wear eclectic items in an unusual way. I know a lady who likes sparkle and glitz. She wears it often and this is her "trademark." She is known and accepted for this. Years ago, there was a woman in Cincinnati who was known for her hats. No one was wearing hats to luncheons or shopping at the time. She didn't care. She wore them anyway.

Nancy

Rules can't be applied. Especially to something so highly personalized.

I suspect one could discuss the rules of appropriate dress, but not of personal style.

What rules?

Jay

People think that only the young (even worse—"the skinny") can break rules and be experimental. Unfortunately, as some people age, they stop searching for newness and cease learning about life. Quite the opposite should be in effect. People start to idealize or hang onto a past lesson of what they perceive as "good" without the spirit or need to evolve. Hopefully, the young and old and "not-so-skinny," will approach dressing/decorating, and conducting themselves with a taste for personal evolution and not for "rule-following."

Yes!

Liz

The only way to make new rules is to break the old ones. Some do not even acknowledge that there are rules.

Absolutely.

Craig

Think of designers!

7

Is it true that if you keep your clothes long enough, they will

Joyce

Some trends do reappear.

For instance, animal print comes and goes. I have a great leopard belt that I pull out periodically when the trend is back. I have seen animal prints in silks, wools, and leathers appear, disappear, and reappear. Often trends reappear with a twist, not exactly the way they were originally designed.

Nancy

Well-made classics and certain "works of art" stand the test of time.

Fashion is gently nudged or nuanced as it recurs and looks dated when resurrected unless it's outstanding to begin with. What should you save? Items you are crazy about because they are "you." Things with good memories or good bones. Stuff you paid dearly for or that makes you laugh.

Jay

Style goes on.

Things can definitely look tired if you hold on too tightly to the past, especially if you identify with the way you used to dress/look. Once you hit 25 and have a job, invest in a few great items that are versatile and functional. If you're 28 and you haven't started, shame on you. Avoid trendy fast fashion stores. The items usually fall apart within weeks. Try to buy what you love without regard to price or label, and buy less. Then, you have investment items

come back in style?

that you could potentially wear forever. Investment items are not always expensive with designer labels. They are items at prices that work in a person's lifestyle.

I find that you can find interesting trendy jewelry items that aren't too expensive, but I believe strongly in really good quality shoes and bags. Cheap bags are a problem and I can't tolerate "fakes." Carrying a fake designer bag indicates a pathetic need for an image. A label doesn't deliver style, success, or self-worth. Real personal style extends into all areas of life, especially the home. I hate going to someone's home expecting it to be great because the owner dresses so well… only to find that clothes are a façade. Buying clothing to the expense of all else limits true personal style.

Liz

Yes.

If it's good, it's good.

Craig

Everything old that comes back has a new way of being old.

Everything changes and time is dynamic. Your style and wardrobe should also be dynamic; however, beautiful pieces last much longer than those that are trendy or poor quality.

Is a simple black dress always in good taste?

Joyce

A simple black dress is the best investment you can make.

Why? It's so versatile and can be coordinated in many ways, with scarves, belts, jewelry, jackets, sweaters. A simple black dress, with or without sleeves, is always in good taste and adaptable to any occasion. Fabrics and styling differ with price.

Nancy

Not by itself.

It is only the backdrop from which to develop a sensational look.

Jay

No.

I have seen a lot of bad black dresses. I call it the Audrey Hepburn syndrome—it was an idea that grew bigger than it needed to and then no one knew what happened. Audrey Hepburn looked great in *Breakfast at Tiffany's,* but she was wearing Givenchy in the film and Hubert de Givenchy was her good friend. He knew what looked great on her and it was custom-fitted so it's not exactly fair to say because it was plain and black that it was in "good taste." It wasn't just the dress that people fell in love with either. It was the character's personality and the way the clothing felt in the scheme of the movie. Now I wish that dress had been the most dreadful color of orange and made of ruffles. If that was the case, I wonder if this question would read: Is a ruffled orange dress always in good taste? The answer might surprise you!

Liz

Yes.

A simple black dress is about creating an impression with a shape. It is straight-forward and personal.

Craig

Always.

Unless, you're getting married.

Who are some of the icons, past or present, that you feel

Joyce

Jackie Kennedy, Princess Diana, Audrey Hepburn, and Chanel.

I like their individuality and their appropriateness. They looked like they enjoyed fashion. Today, I like the way Michelle Obama dresses. She has her own style. She wears both expensive and inexpensive clothing and puts her own personal stamp on her outfits.

Nancy

I have a great affinity for the *jolie-laide* (pretty/ugly).

Like those style-makers who are not traditionally beautiful—Chanel, Schiaparelli, Wallis Simpson, and Diana Vreeland. I'm personally drawn to their lavish use of accessories.

Jay

A list of favorites.

Willem DeKooning: He could wear a suit with the same ease he wore his flannel shirts and wool cardigans.

Carine Roitfeld: She has the ability to always look completely appropriate, sensual, and untouchable. She exudes a very natural energy for life and you never know what designer she is wearing because she always looks like herself and picks according to what she likes as opposed to over-editorialized clothes.

Cate Blanchett: She seems to have fun with clothes and never looks like the clothes are wearing her.

have great style?

A list of favorites.

James Dean: I have never seen a pea coat look better on anyone!

Björk: She has respect for clothes as a creative outlet and does not limit herself with public perception and rules. I always get the feeling she is in love with everything she puts on herself and uses each outfit to express a facet of her personality. I find the reaction to her so fascinating too, since people are quick to say how crazy she is.

Stefano Pilati: I think he is the most stylish man and approaches everything with a great balance of humor and honor. He seems to have a very honest, touchable quality to his work as well as the way he conducts himself.

Liz

Grace Coddington: She reminds me of a clean pencil sketch, without any evidence of hesitation or complication. Not only does her style come through in her uniform but also in the images she creates. She captures the integrity of the idea behind the design and adds her own narrative to the image. She encourages me to see my environment as something I can define to suit me.

Camilla Nickerson: Her highly intellectual work has inspired my concept development on several projects. She is always doing something new and making new connections that raise the level of respect the viewer has for clothing. I like people who take fashion seriously enough to experiment with it and she does that to the nth degree. Everything she does is well thought out, as is her style. She once said, "I think if you promote your mind outward, constantly questioning, constantly looking, and constantly informing your world, then you have style. You can show you are healthy and exciting, if you can get it together. My style tip is: 'TRY A BIT HARDER!'"

Melanie Ward: I identify a great deal with Melanie Ward. When I see her work, I get it. When I read about her past work, I laugh because she "stole" my ideas. She harmoniously combines classic sophistication with unusual details. She uses very forward and modern pieces in the most natural way, creating irony without being too symbolic. Her work is provocative because it questions paradoxes by denying their existence.

Linda Rodin: Linda is beautiful. She has this ethereal quality, yet she is the most down-to-earth stylist I have ever met. Not only her personal style, but also the way she styles others, has taught me that elegance is the intellectual twist on sexy. She showed me that you could be sexy, fun, and edgy but still be sophisticated, minimal, and serious. Linda's style strikes a balance between natural beauty and taking risks. She demands respect and admiration, yet she is honest and approachable. Although I have only had the pleasure of meeting her a handful of times, I consider her an icon for everything fabulous about reality.

Penelope Tree: In a recent interview for *style.com* Penelope said, "People thought I was a freak and I kind of liked that. I felt I was an alien so I didn't see anything wrong with looking like one." That quote says it all. I've always been intrigued by the fact that when people told her she didn't look like a model, she responded by emphasizing the "strangest element of herself,"—her eyes. She provoked people to consider her perspective on beauty and changed the industry's concept of beauty as a result. Penelope Tree proves that style is about being true to you. She said, "You can't look like *Vogue*. It doesn't want you to. It just wants to show you what individuality is."

Craig

From the stage and silver screen.

Greta Garbo, Marlena Deitrich, Princess Grace, Cher, Jennifer Lopez, Angelina Jolie.

10

Can you change your style?

Joyce

Yes, out of boredom or a change in circumstances.

Periodically, people become bored with their way of dressing and want to change their looks. This can be done in so many ways with a new hairstyle, emphasizing a different color in a wardrobe, and being more aware of what is current. Perhaps you lost a great deal of weight. Here is a wonderful opportunity to change your style. You may have entered the work world. Again, another chance to reevaluate your clothing choices.

Nancy

I think, probably not.

You can change your clothing or cut your hair, etc., but it doesn't work to change one's core. I do believe, however, that style can and should evolve with exposure, lifestyle, and age.

Jay

Never a 180, but yes, people evolve and tastes change.

It's great to play and experiment as long as at the core you have the foundation of something that always makes you look like "you." It could be a silhouette, a fragrance that you always wear, a haircut that is distinctive to you. As long as some thread of you remains constant, you should feel free to play. It's obscene to say that your style will not change—that something is "not your thing," etc. This idea frustrates me very much!

Liz

I wouldn't use the word change.

Change implies separating from the past and becoming something new. I prefer "evolve." You can evolve your style over time. It's a matter of words. By all means, experiment and find new ways of expressing yourself, but don't try to become an idea that isn't your own.

Craig

Absolutely and you should.

It may be the same style, but it should always be up to date with the changes that reflect who you are today, not yesterday.

Wardrobe

"Give a girl the right pair of shoes
and she can conquer the world."

—Bette Midler

11

What are the essential pieces you should purchase when

Build around a neutral.

Joyce

If starting from scratch, I would suggest the following purchases based on a best neutral color in a year-round fabric: pant suit with a matching skirt, a cardigan, a white shirt, a basic slipover sweater, a short casual coat, a long coat, a rain coat, an extra jacket. A larger handbag for day, a smaller one for evening, and a dressier one for fancy occasions. Professional women may have specific wardrobe needs.

It seems one discusses "wardrobe development" when life is in transition.

Nancy

The need seems to arise, most importantly, when young women move from campus to professional life. In that case, I would suggest buying a beautiful suit in a best neutral color. Buy the best quality that you can afford. It would be wonderful to buy three pieces: jacket, skirt, and trousers. Then build off the base. Thirty years ago, I worked for Casual Corner. This is when women were first entering the job market in great numbers. They had a formula that made sense: two (suits), plus two (bottoms), plus five (tops) equals 30 "looks"—a month's worth of changes. That formula is still good. However, you can really make this happen with a base of one beautiful suit. Picture a wonderful black suit. Then, play off the basics. Add a black and white tweed skirt. Consider a pinstriped trouser. Purchase a

developing a general wardrobe?

great white shirt, a black cashmere sweater, black and white tees, and perhaps some color. Change looks with a broad range of accessories, etc.

Jay

» Pants in two silhouettes: slim and wide.
» A men's oxford shirt: they look amazing on all sizes and darts on the women's oxford shirts are not sexy. You can wear them oversized with leggings, if you are large on top. You can tuck and wrap them if you have a tiny waist (and big or small chest). You can wear them open if you have a flat chest. You can roll the sleeves up and down to change the proportion of your body. You can wear any color and it's almost never gross. If you're married to a man or date guys (or even if you're a woman dating a woman), you can almost always find one in your, his, or her closet—FREE! Please don't knot them.
» Lightweight and heavyweight coat/jacket with classic styling (probably in cashmere— no point in buying something cheap if you want it to last you a long time). Good coats and jackets work easily over all wardrobes. A chic jacket can even tone down a gown.
» A dress that you love in black or a color that makes you feel chic.
» Pull on stretch skirt—especially if you have hips.

Liz

» Pants—casual and formal. You can always layer and play with tops, turn them upside down, unbutton, fold...whatever you want, but your lower half is a bit more boring. Your legs must move and you have to cover up, so find a few good reliable pairs of pants. Get at least two silhouettes—one skinny and casual (showing off the leg) and one wide with a good sturdy waist which adds emphasis and changes the whole silhouette of whatever you put on top.

» Oversized but quality shirts. Nothing with bad seams/darts. If it is oversized, you can tuck it in, belt, wear open, as a dress half tucked in, backwards. Endless opportunities to be creative but looks clean too.

» "That dress."—The one that you can throw on and change up with different accessories.

» "The dress."—The one that makes you excited and want to wake up in the morning. The one that allows you to check off fabulous for that week. Or cure a case of seasonal depression. You must get "the dress."

» Shorts! There are so many kinds. Sheer chiffon are my favorite, but you could also try ruffled, lace, men's, leather, high-waisted, bubble, drop-crotch, denim, even khaki. Shorts can be more practical than a skirt to show off legs, but avoid American Apparel spandex booty shorts. Not cute.

Craig

Essentials are basic pieces that can be built upon and accessorized to be functional and elegant. The essential pieces are: the key black dress, knit dress, jacket, skirt and pant, a white blouse, black and white short sleeved t-shirts, a cashmere sweater, and a scarf/shawl. Items should play back to one another and be easily added to with individual pieces to be exciting, seasonal, elegant, or professional.

12

What types of coats would you recommend for a

Joyce

Four essentials.

A long coat, a short sporty coat, a raincoat, a casual jacket.

Nancy

Just two.

I think I could get by with two coats, again in a "best" neutral. A perfect coat would be a cashmere, camel hair, or alpaca A-shaped (or swing) coat with raglan sleeves—allowing you to layer. In the right color/fabric combinations, it could work for evening. The second would be a rain repellent coat, either a classic trench or again an A shape.

Jay

Wrap trench coats in cotton or cashmere.

Single or double breasted—preferably waterproof (cashmere comes backed with waterproof membranes now too).

general wardrobe?

A trenchcoat.

**One for all
weathers.**

Liz
A trench is the best transitional coat.

Craig
An all weather car coat, raincoat, or stylish trench that can be worn to work and out in the evening.

13

How would you describe a basic jewelry wardrobe that would

Pearls and more.

Joyce

I love pearls of any kind—authentic or fashion. I would suggest some ropes of pearls in white or mixed colors, a 15 inch pearl necklace, and pearl earrings, both long and button type. You can't own enough pearls. They are right for day and evening. Additionally, I suggest a gold 15 inch chain and a longer one that can be doubled. One of my very favorite necklaces is a long lightweight link chain that I wear long as well as looped twice. Gold earrings that dangle, as well as perhaps a knot. I also like hoops. The same pieces in silver would look great with gray. If you wear a significant earring, I would suggest no necklace. A nice watch either in gold or mixed gold and silver. A statement pin is also good to have in your wardrobe. For evening you, of course, can wear the pearls but you might like something sparklier.

Costume jewelry is my thing.

Nancy

But, if I were interested in building a "fine" jewelry wardrobe, I would first purchase a good watch and hoop earrings in the same metal. Then, I would add a long strand of pearls, and purchase an armload of bangles

offer choices for work as well as dressier occasions?

even if one at a time. Eventually, add stones. Don't be afraid to mix real with fake for a bigger look. I would rather buy jewelry than any other wardrobe item, and never want fine jewelry. I can't buy it big enough to suit my tastes, and it's just too precious for my wardrobe.

Jay

Giant diamonds.

Perfect for work, grocery shopping, and dinner. I am not kidding. If you have less money— smaller diamonds. Always, amazing bracelets. Bracelets are the one thing that, no matter how inexpensive look amazing. I recommend wearing lots on one wrist (or both if you're adventurous). A woman in a classic men's watch is always so sexy and smart looking. It looks great at work, soccer games, and with a cocktail dress.

Liz

Rings!

Hands are sexy and powerful. A big ring or a bunch of rings—doesn't matter as long as they work together and look natural on your hand. If I had diamonds, I would wear them. Simple diamond studs are amazing and work for every occasion. A big diamond ring. Also, bangles can be worn singularly and look beautiful mixed (but you have to have a lot). Unless necklaces are really innovative and weird, they don't really do much for me. They can take away too much from an outfit. I wear the same

"A woman in a classic men's watch is always so sexy and smart looking."

jewelry almost every day. One big black onyx ring on the left hand and three to five simple silver rings that I would call small, but others would find big. The amount of rings isn't crazy, because they all work together. Then, I have a simple silver necklace (a good one) and a silver/onyx cuff. It all works together easily and can become the focus of my outfit or can be invisible depending on what I'm wearing.

Diamonds.

Craig

The basic pieces of jewelry should be diamond and/or pearl studs, a great forever watch, pearls, and a removable diamond pendant. Basic and timeless investment pieces can be worn most anywhere.

14

Do you believe in shopping for clothes and accessories at less

I shop in all types of stores.

Joyce

I find very often the best shawls, scarves, and belts that I own are from less expensive stores. You need to be focused and not buy something if you don't know specifically how it works into your wardrobe.

Absolutely...this is the way of the contemporary world.

Nancy

Spend well. Spend wisely on basic, seasonless pieces, but don't be afraid to mix these investments with new things. Trendy items and accessories can be well-bought in less expensive spots. Keep an eye out for neat construction and natural fabrics when buying less expensive clothing items. I remember reading an article a few years ago when Karl Lagerfeld talked about his "girls" mixing their Chanel pieces with articles from H&M. As I recall, he advised buying at high and low ends and skipping the middle (bridge) product. That makes sense to me.

expensive stores?

Jay

Yes, and NOT
because of the
economy.

There are bad clothes and accessories in expensive stores too. Don't give yourself too much credit for getting a bargain though, unless you REALLY love it, and wanted it all along! Don't buy an item just because it's cheap, or just because it's "designer."

Liz

Of course!

But don't fill your closet with "two-fers" and "as-is" deals.

Craig

Cost vs Quality.

For core wardrobe pieces that are seasonless, it is better to buy higher quality that will last longer. Trendy colors, cuts and designs can be bought with "fashion for a price" attitudes without the guilt. Mix the less expensive pieces with your better or designer pieces—focus on your style and plan out your most expensive purchases first.

15

Must you always buy a complete outfit when shopping?

Joyce

It is a good idea to try to complete one outfit before moving on to another.

This doesn't mean you need to purchase new shoes or a handbag for each outfit. You may already have appropriate ones in your wardrobe. Mentally, though, go through what you own and what you need to finish the new outfit. Ask yourself: "Do I need to buy or do I already own the right shoes, handbag, blouse, sweater, accessories to make this look work?" This prevents you from "having a lot of clothes and nothing to wear."

Nancy

Not at all.

Special items can be added and worn in a variety of ways with existing pieces. I don't think I've ever bought a complete outfit, and hardly ever put outfits together in the same way.

Jay

No. Disgusting.

I DO believe in buying several pieces that go together and that work back to many things in your wardrobe. If you only buy one item to go with one other item, then shame on you.

Liz

Funny...don't think I can remember the last time I did that.

If I ever want an "outfit" the way it's marketed, chances are I would have to take out a loan to get it. I don't usually pair pieces of the same brand. Every company has their specialty in my closet. If we are talking Prada, however, I'll take it in its perfect form right off the mannequin and I'll make it fit.

Craig

Sometimes.

If you like what you see as a complete outfit, buy the complete outfit, especially if you need to match color.

16

Would you buy a trend because it is "in style," even if you don't

No.

Joyce

Never.

My quick answer is "no," but my modified answer is a little different.

Nancy

Sometimes, at its early introduction, I will consider a "trend" and reject it but eventually my eye will adapt to the item. I have a growing sense of appreciation. An example would be extreme trouser silhouettes—harem pants, suspenders, extra high waists, etc.

No.

Liz

I wouldn't.

like the trend.

Personally, no.

Jay

For others, if it's a proportion you believe in even though you know it's "trendy," then I say yes. A proportion can always be taken in, let out, hemmed, layered differently, and taken up or down.

Love it or leave it.

Craig

Never buy anything you don't love or you're not comfortable wearing. It will be the item in your closet that sits with the tags on it forever! If a trend lasts over time, it becomes a style and may be worth considering at a future time.

What items should a classic style-type add to her wardrobe

Try new color combinations.

Joyce

Pair red with brown, brown with navy. Purchase a new every day bag. Add a jacket in a new color, pattern, or texture to slacks or a skirt already in your closet. You may want to add a new lower heeled shoe.

Break rules, but not all of them at once.

Nancy

Go for an updated silhouette in a neutral color, or a fashion-forward color in a classic silhouette.

Designer shoes that are slightly uncomfortable to walk in, but you can "work it out" in!

Jay

That is one trick! Shoes always seem to take an outfit somewhere new, plus they change your proportion. If your shoes are mildly uncomfortable, but you can bear it, you know you are doing the right thing. Also, you can buy shoes a half size big and get insoles. That is something no one really tells you. I do it and I can run around the city each day wearing shoes that should be really uncomfortable (would do it in heels too). Try Alaïa shoes—high and comfortable! I forgot to mention, an Hermès bag!

to look more updated?

Two things.

Liz

1. Amazing SHOES!!! Crazy shoes that change your whole look, but that you can still walk in (at least for the first hour). **2.** A big piece of jewelry that can stand on its own, like my ridiculous onyx ring. I can't live without it.

New special items.

Craig

Designers use cuts, draping, color, and lengths as key elements to define the vision of the collection. A new style top is always the easiest and fastest item to update your skirts and slacks. The next piece would be the jacket that can be worn to update a dress or alter an outfit.

18

What would you suggest for a basic handbag wardrobe?

Joyce

Build around one neutral.

Again, I would suggest a new handbag wardrobe to be based around one main color. This way you can buy better quality bags and less of them. For instance, if black is your main color, purchase a larger black day bag, a smaller black bag for evening, and a black silk bag for dressier occasions. This eliminates the need to purchase brown, navy, gray, etc. Interesting that I find red to be a neutral color that goes with almost everything. After buying the three bags above, the fourth could be red.

Nancy

Match your leather to your hair.

Choose a shape that is "neat," but not too structured so that it is adaptable for work and casual. Again, purchase it in your best neutral color. Someone told me that if you can only afford one shoe/bag color, you should match the leather to your hair! Think about it—it just may work. The other "must" is a satin evening bag. If your summer wardrobe includes a lot of white or light colors, you'll need a third bag that works with that palette. A good choice is a metallic bag in the same color as most of the jewelry you wear. Finally, if you need a bag for your laptop, buy the best you can afford in leather or nylon. I would buy it in my "best" neutral color.

Hermès.

Jay

I would not say black and basic either. The right one would work all the time.

Liz

One perfect dream bag for day and a small bag for evening.

I wish I could tell you I have it, but I'm still looking. It has to be perfect. I only recently decided that yes, I would pay $1,000+ for the perfect bag. It has be able to take a beating though, and age well. I don't like big for evening. Really big bags are so frustrating for me, because I can't afford the ones I want, like the Prada fringe bag from 2008 or the Fendi peek-a-boo bag. Both amazing bags that wear well. For evening, I like clutches. Usually with jewels or metal. A simple metal clutch can be fabulous. In general I prefer structure for night.

Basic colors.

Craig

Basic colors of black, brown, or neutral in styles that can be worn for day or evening whenever possible.

19

Why do stores have summer clothing arriving in February

Joyce

I too always thought this so odd.

When I want a summer dress in June, the stores are showing winter things. This situation is because designing and manufacturing is done about 6 months ahead of the season. I personally think the best summer things, however, come in to the stores in January and the best winter things arrive in June.

Nancy

The industry is built around this pattern.

To receive shipping from the best vendors, store buyers have to abide by the standard. One of my favorite designers, Donna Karan. is trying to get designers and retailers to rethink the strategy. It's not smart. By the time most clients want seasonal items, they are marked down. The calendar really devalues the designer and frustrates the client. When I buy something, I want to wear it now, not in three months.

Jay

It's the fashion cycle.

I think ultimately it comes from two points: People don't live in the present; they don't buy what they need, but they get bored with the cold and they want things that remind them of warm. They get bored with warm and they want things that remind them of

and winter clothing arriving in June? It seems so odd.

cold. If it were warm and there were shorts in the store, people wouldn't buy them because they would say, "I don't really need these. The ones I am wearing are perfectly fine," or "I'll wait till they go on sale," which retailers don't like. However, it seems the best part about this cycle is that when you need the item, it will be on sale, even heavily on sale. But then, you don't get the full season's wear out of it. Fashion is pushed by retailers to get things in to the stores faster and faster, which is making product arrive earlier than normal.

People purchase clothing based on what they want over what they need for the most part.

Liz

Shopping is a luxury, so people want to fantasize about what they will wear to that party or when the weather changes or when they lose five pounds. It is rare that you will want to buy something similar to what you are wearing. The only way to sell is to sell the future or the image of the future. This is just the way we are. We like to plan for the future. It makes us feel secure to be prepared. Also, I don't think many people even follow the season rule anymore. You can layer in the winter or throw a coat over whatever you are wearing. I wear shorts in the winter with leggings.

"The best summer things, come into the stores in January and the best winter things arrive in June."

Collective Fashion Wisdom

Marketing determines assortment.

Craig

It seems so odd, but marketing strategies encourage consumers to buy at key periods. Pre-season arrives early for those who plan ahead, travel, and may want first choice of the inventory. If the buyers have vendors ship Spring in February, it's because they assume you are done buying for the Winter season, and if you see collections that are refreshing and exciting, you will start buying for the next season.

20

Are there any fashion guidelines for women over fifty?

The guidelines for good taste apply to any age.

Joyce

Dressing simply with good fabrics, an appropriate skirt length, and flattering colors are all things to be considered. Also, a person's figure at 50+ must be addressed. At this time, a woman might wish to wear long sleeves or three-quarter length sleeves instead of sleeveless things. When you look in the mirror after dressing and have doubts, change your clothes.

I think there is age-appropriate dressing, but it's so hard to generalize.

Nancy

Some mature women can work youthful items well. I think the best advice is to avoid anything too tight or too revealing. Wear clothing that draws attention to what's still good, and detracts from what is not so good.

No.

Jay

Depends on what their bodies look like but overall, no.

No.

Liz

Working in a vintage store has taught me that everyone makes his own rules and the older one is, the cooler the rules could possibly get.

Lines and lengths!

Craig

Consider the lines that are most flattering and watch hem lengths and plunging necklines. Keep it young, but tasteful, and don't try to wear the same things you wore when you were in your twenties or thirties! It is much sexier to see someone classic, sophisticated, and stylish with confidence!

Color

"I found I could say things with color and shapes that I couldn't say any other way—things I had no words for."
—Georgia O'Keefe

21

Can one mix neutrals; that is, black with navy?

**You can easily
mix neutrals.**

Joyce

For some, this may be a stretch at first,
but neutral combinations can be very sophisticated. Start with one dominant color and use
the secondary color with accessories such as
shoes, scarves, or handbags. I like neutral
mixing very much, and think the end result is
quite interesting.

Very chic.

Nancy

Consider all of the basic neutrals: black,
brown, gray, navy, beige, and camel. All can
be worn in tandem. Black and brown; black
and gray, black and navy, black and beige,
black and camel, and so on.

PLEASE do.

Jay

These are the color combinations I wear daily.
It's SO old fashioned to think you can't wear
black and navy or black and brown. These
kinds of "rules" really hurt fashion and are
ill-conceived.

Navy with brown? Gray with brown?

Liz

Meant to be mixed. But that doesn't mean they can be used interchangeably. Neutrals share similar properties. You have to learn that sometimes the result of mixing neutrals looks purposeful, and other times it looks like an accident. If you look "gray," but you aren't wearing gray, you have muted yourself by mixing neutrals that are too similar. Think more about value than color. Light gray with navy blue looks great, but dark gray with navy blue looks awkward.

Craig

Definitely. Black is great with brown, gray, etc. Look at what colors look best on you and don't be afraid to try something new. Look at magazines and store displays for ideas on how mix color.

22   Can one mix blacks?

Mixing blacks can have definite fashion value.

Joyce

I like wearing different tones of black together. I also like wearing different black fabric textures together. Woven fabrics with flat fabrics, satin with wool, and wool with velvet are just a few examples that work very well when combined. A few pieces in different black tones and textures immensely increase the capacity of your wardrobe opportunities.

Blacks can be mixed with care.

Nancy

I think garments' "blackness" needs to be of the same depth. If the blacks are of the same density, a variety of textures pulled together in black look sensational.

This depends.

Jay

Washing black items can definitely create a problem. When black garments have been worn or washed too much and are worn together with other black items, they sometimes look ratty and cheap—more "grayed out" than black. Also, different fibers take dye differently. What is "black" in one garment can sometimes look "dirty black" in another.

I would avoid trying to wear too many versions of the same color because the end result can end up looking muddy and frustrated. However, I don't mind mixing tonalities of black or "uncolor" colors like dark, dark charcoal, or deep navy (that looks almost black). When these colors are paired with black, the subtlety of the other color pops. I don't think anyone should ever wear black head to toe unless it's a black dress, or the black is finished with incredible accessories. It's kind of an outdated idea that chic people only wear black. Plus, black reads as unapproachable. That's why most uniforms are navy, brown, or gray.

Liz

Create your own palette of blacks.

Mixing blacks is the best way to have "a lot going on" without being obvious about it. Mixing warm and cool blacks can be a good way to layer things and add different values to your ensemble. Also everything comes in black so you can have an incredibly diverse collection of black pieces made of different fabrics and with different textures, lengths, styles, detail, and sheerness that you can mix and match to create new looks. Mixing blacks is what I do.

Craig

Mixing blacks is easiest when they are textured.

Two different blacks are okay when they are the same tonal blacks, i.e., don't mix a reddish brown black with a grayed out black.

23

How can one gain confidence when mixing colors and textures?

Joyce

Lighten up.

Fashion is often taken too seriously. Trying various color and texture combinations can be lots of fun. Try new combinations on weekends first. When you have more confidence, wear your creation to work. Observe what other people wear and how they dress. What is the worst thing that could happen to you by taking a chance and wearing a new combination once?

Nancy

The key is accessories.

If one is wearing a black, gray, camel, or navy dress, for instance, and perhaps adds chocolate brown shoes and a mink collar—she's created pure glamour. It could be much simpler though. Think of a gray skirt with brown shoes and tortoiseshell glasses. Scarves are under-worn in the US and are a clever tool for relating unrelated colors. Scarves often incorporate a sophisticated blend of colors. Begin with the scarf and add hard pieces that appear within the color range of the scarf. Jewelry can be used in the same way. A navy dress with jet beads and patent oxfords is a sophisticated combination. Try a black dress and load on silver jewelry and finish with gray shoes. I could go on…

Dress like a work of art.

Jay

Dress like a work of art. Look at paintings by Mark Rothko, Monet, Degas, DeKoonig. Look at photos by Robert Polidori. Inspire yourself.

Contrast is important.

Liz

If something seems too shiny, too yellow, too large, then balance it out with an opposite.

Keep looking.

Craig

If you don't have an eye for color, read fashion magazines, look at store displays, and stick to a basic palette. Look online and download a color block to see what colors work together and what colors clash. When shopping, hold the clothes up to your face in a mirror and see what you love. More often than not, your best colors are those that you are personally drawn to in general.

24

Is there a place for several neutral colors in one wardrobe, or should

Joyce

There is definitely room for more than one neutral grouping in a wardrobe.

If, however, you are on a limited budget, you may want to limit your color selection to just one neutral. It is more economical to work with one color and the easiest one to work with is black. You can always add to black after you've selected your main pieces. You will need only one good handbag in black and a pair of high and low heels. You can also easily add sale pieces after you have collected a sizeable grouping of whatever base color you choose, and then begin working on another neutral color grouping.

Nancy

Black for life.

If you love clothing and have a good budget for clothing purchases, by all means, have as many neutrals as you like in your closet. But if you want to be smart, cost effective, and streamlined, build your wardrobe around your best neutral. No question, I could live with only black. I have most neutrals in my closet, but I almost wish I didn't. Excitement, for me, comes with accessories.

Jay

Several.

If you are a very specific person—then it's great to have one color and build against it. For example, I don't like the way black looks on me, and I never wear it. I work everything around navy and gray, but I think this is more

one work with one neutral and build against it?

easily accomplished in menswear. If I were a woman, I would probably feel differently about buying black clothes. I would totally rock black and all the other neutrals and feel amazing about it.

Liz

Of course, you can have several neutrals.

Color can be overwhelming, and if you like to layer, it is easier to do so with neutrals. Just build a collection of neutrals in different fabrics and weights so that your wardrobe does not become one singular value. Remember that you can add some of your own coloring through sheer materials to make more natural colors.

Craig

Change for the time of day or year.

Build on more than one neutral so you have variety and to keep your wardrobe exciting. You will most likely enjoy having different neutrals for day and evening and the change of seasons.

25

I love black, but know it is harsh. How can I soften it up?

Joyce

Use color next to your face with scarves and jewelry.

Wear a jacket in another color over black to "lighten up" the total feel. Navy is an alternative to black, especially midnight blue.

Nancy

You only need to soften around the face.

Try a nude, light pink, buff, or cream collar, blouse, scarf, or jewelry. Certain fabrics (like chiffon and certain silks) are also much softer than others, even when they are black. Beautiful makeup and the right hair can also help tremendously.

Jay

With charming personality and wit...and a smile.

Wear it in chiffon with soft, neutral make-up, a fun, colorful shoe and sleek hair.

Liz

Pay attention to the details.

Black can be intimidating because it's mysterious—it's the uncolor. The best way to combat the starkness of black is to vary the weight, shine, hue, and texture of the fabric. Black can look too unnatural and separate from you if you don't pay attention to details.

Craig

Add color and tone.

Wearing tones of black will help—gray is softer than black. Framing your face with a white collar or pearls makes you look alert. Adding red lips or a scarf adds excitement. Use your layers to bring in color. Keep the jacket in black and wear a top in another color.

26

How do I know which colors look best on me?

Joyce

Three methods.

Consult a professional. Most retail clothing stores have professionals available to you at no cost. Seek their unbiased opinion. They are trained to know how to advise you. Take a trusted friend shopping with you. Someone whose opinion you value. Go to a fabric store alone or with someone else and just hold up lots of different fabrics to your face. Look in the mirror and see what looks best.

Nancy

Skin undertones tell you a lot.

Some of us are "warm" with yellow or orange undertones to the skin and others of us are "cool" with blue or red undertones. Do you look better in orange-red or blue-red? If the answer is orange-red, you'll look good in a warm color palette. If the answer is blue-red, you'll look great in cool color palettes. *Color Me Beautiful*, a concept book from the 80's, always worked. Several times I was used as a "model" in front of an audience. Every time the consultant draped a funny green color around my neck, the audience told me that I looked great. I was stunned. The result was that I was a "spring," and could wear soft warm colors the best. I don't dress that way now, but I know those colors flatter me. When I wear them I get compliments. A simple thing to do is to go to a really good makeup artist. Ask him/her to apply a soft complementary palette that suits your skin and that you could wear daily. See if you end up in warm or cool colors and go from there. Another thing is to tune in when you get compliments. Do people tell you that you look great every time you wear an old red sweater? There's probably a reason. Remember to listen to the times you're told "You look great," not to the times you're told "I love your sweater!"

Jay

Honesty.

Ask your best friend and be willing to accept constructive criticism. It's a little like bad breath; you are so happy someone pulled you aside and handed you a stick of gum. If that doesn't work, find a mirror and be honest with yourself.

"It's a little like bad breath; you are so happy someone pulled you aside and handed you a stick of gum."

Liz

Achieve balance through contrast.

Just like choosing your makeup hue, your goal is to balance out your natural color. If you have a warmer skin tone, then cool colors will look better on you; darker skin, then bright colors look amazing; brown skin is balanced with pastels. If you are very white, then black provides balance. We have a natural desire to balance things. The best way to bring out your unique coloring is through contrast. A green-eyed person in a green dress always looks great, but wouldn't it be even better if a green-eyed red-head wore the dress? Opposites attract for a reason.

Craig

Consult a mirror or a professional.

Look in the mirror under different lighting and hold different colors next to your face. Use fabrics, makeup, magazines or anything that holds true color next to your skin. The colors that you love are generally your true colors. You can always have a makeover in the cosmetics department and they will help you with color. If you have a personal shopper, they will help you with color.

27

Is it appropriate to wear black to a wedding? What about wearing

Joyce

Modern thinking obliterates rules.

Black is now fine for weddings. In fact, black is often worn by bridesmaids. In the past, people thought black was too depressing to wear to a happy occasion. Today, it is widely acceptable. White can also be worn at weddings. Previously, it was thought that if you wore white to a wedding, you were competing with the bride. It was her day and she should be the only one in white. Today, brides often wear pastel wedding dresses.

Nancy

Black, but white?

I am very comfortable with black at weddings, especially when they are cocktail or formal events. Black is chic, appropriate, and even if you're gorgeous, the bride will still be the center of attention. Think sophisticated, not gothic black though. Weddings are soft affairs, not stark. White worries me. It's the bride's deal, but it could work if well selected. A simple white dress or tuxedo may work. I'm not really picturing it though.

white to a wedding?

Jay

**Black—yes;
White—yes.**

Part of me wants to write "no" to white on this question, but I don't think brides should only consider white for a wedding. I know many people wouldn't agree, but I feel it's so old fashioned to say white is only for the bride and not for guests. Whatever you wear, look smoking hot because chances are the bride won't look that good anyway...not your fault.

Liz

With consideration.

Weddings are difficult as you want to look nice, but you don't want to stand out. I think black is a good choice as long as you don't look too heavy. Black isn't a sad color unless it overpowers you. White is okay as well. Just add some non-white accessories. Don't wear a veil and you'll be okay.

Craig

White may give them something to talk about.

If the event is black tie or evening or the bride announces that black is acceptable, you can wear black. White is still on hold for the bride unless you prefer to cause a little chatter.

28

Are there still "out-of-season" colors?

Joyce

Personal, seasonal, and local preference.

Most colors are worn year-round. I still find it difficult to wear winter white in the fall. I like the fall shades and lean toward them in Autumn. For the holiday, I pick up winter white. However, you will see white worn throughout the year. Most fabrics are acceptable year round too. You will see suede and leather worn during the summer. Your locale will often determine this.

Nancy

Not at all.

I would say there were out of season fabrics, but not out of season colors. A white wool coat and a baby pink cashmere sweater are particularly beautiful in a deep freeze. I love summer black too.

Jay

No.

Absolutely not.

It depends more on where you live than what season it is.

Not so much.

Liz
If you wear hot pink during a snowstorm in NYC, it's a bit more noticeable than if you were in Texas on a temperate February afternoon.

Craig
In general, pastels are still for spring/summer, but when worn as an accessory with a dark color, they are still acceptable. The weight and the climate may dictate color more than fashion rules. Never have rules been made to be broken as much as with fashion!

29

When interviewing for a job, what color(s) do you suggest wearing?

Joyce

Dark colors are more credible.

When selecting an outfit for interviewing, keep the outfit simple. You do not want your clothing or jewelry to detract from the interview. Dark colors are the most credible. Stick to neutrals of some type. Both skirts and pantsuits are acceptable. Clothing can be more expressive if you are interviewing for a fashion, marketing, or creative position.

Nancy

Be yourself.

Wear your best neutral, but wear it in a way that reveals personal style. No cookie cutter interview suits. Unique individuals wanted for hire.

Jay

Not gender neutral.

Men—navy or gray. Women—as long as it's not a poly blend ill-fitting suit, you can interview in whatever color you want. Wear amazing shoes, though.

Liz

Go with neutrals.

Take more chances with accessories than with your outfit because accessories can be a fun way of dressing up and showing personal style without looking inappropriate or obvious. You want to look serious and clean. Also the goal of the interview should be to get to know who you are not how you dress. So, neutrals are a good choice, as they don't distract.

Craig

Industry specific choices.

It depends on the career, but you want to focus on a conservative and understated wardrobe. Base your outfit on a successful person within the company or industry in which you are interviewing.

30

Are there any color combinations that are taboo today?

Joyce

Color combinations are very personal.

Some are more pleasant to the eye than others but the final decision is individual. When in doubt, change the combination.

Nancy

I don't like the word taboo.

There is always the rare person of style who makes the worst thing in the world look like the best thing in the world. Within specific cultures, however, colors have symbolic meanings and are considered inappropriate at certain times.

Jay

Orange and black are a tough sell to me.

Ralph Lauren has the best cashmere jackets in his store (at the time of this writing) in orange that made me rethink my answer, but when driving past his store on Bleecker yesterday, the beautiful jackets were styled with black tights and pumpkins were in the windows. Now I feel the same way again—gross. "Taboo color" is just such a weird thing to me. Aside from tradition and social significance, there is no reason historically that colors should be considered taboo. If you love it, wear it. Stop worrying about all the perceived rules.

Not taboo, but unattractive.

Liz

All pastels, all primary, all-American, anything too thematic is hard to get away with. It's really important to understand how texture and weight play a huge roll when mixing colors.

Occasion appropriate.

Craig

Certain colors may be taboo for certain places or events, but no color itself is taboo.

Accessories

"If I feel really low, I go to see Philip [Treacy], cover my face [with his hats] and feel fantastic [. . .]. Wearing a hat is like cosmetic surgery."
—**Isabella Blow**

31

Is there a simple way to incorporate accessories into a wardrobe?

Joyce

Begin with a few good pieces.

Scarves, jewelry, and handbags are all accessories. Buy a few good items in each category that can be used with many outfits.

Nancy

Perhaps not so simple.

So many people have told me that they struggle with accessories that I would hesitate to say that accessorizing is simple. For some reason, I keep thinking of Christmas trees. There are "Charlie Brown" trees, trees with little white lights, trees with hand-made ornaments, artificial trees, natural trees, trees with gaudy ornaments and blinking lights, trees fit for the Hall of Mirrors at Versailles. Some of us prefer simplicity, or no adornment, and others have highly decorative styles.

A beautifully draped dress accessorized with only the perfect shoe may stand alone for a minimalist. A classic style-type could add a strand of pearls or a broach at the shoulder and a beautiful watch. Those more comfortable with accessories could choose an arm load of bangles á la Nancy Cunard or a wrapped head á la Big and Little Edies. If you feel that you would like to add accessories, but don't know how, start small, perfect, and classic. Buy diamond studs, a pearl necklace, a Tiffany bracelet, a Hermès scarf. Add one perfect piece at a time. I love the idea of signature accessories like Jackie O sunglasses, Barbara

Bush pearls, or Philip Johnson round spectacles. That's making an accessory statement without really thinking. Look for well-accessorized looks in magazines, catalogues, online, etc. Make a file. Look at it when you're trying to get to sleep. Maybe you'll remember it in the morning and get creative.

Jay

Instinctively or functionally.

Just wear them. Wear a lot or a little. Function is good, too.

Liz

Determine personal purpose.

You can create a group of accessories that you can wear every day. Depends on how you like to use accessories—to add color, status, dress up/down, functionally, or as a focal point. Perhaps you only like jewelry that makes noise, for instance. Once you figure out what purpose accessories serve for you, you can build a collection that serves your purpose.

Craig

Select a focal point.

Know your best body features and always dress and accessorize to keep one of those great areas as your focal point. If defining your waist is best, then accessorize with sensational belts. If your face is your best feature, then wear necklaces, pins high on the shoulder, scarves and/or glasses that frame the face. Focus on a feature, then accessorize.

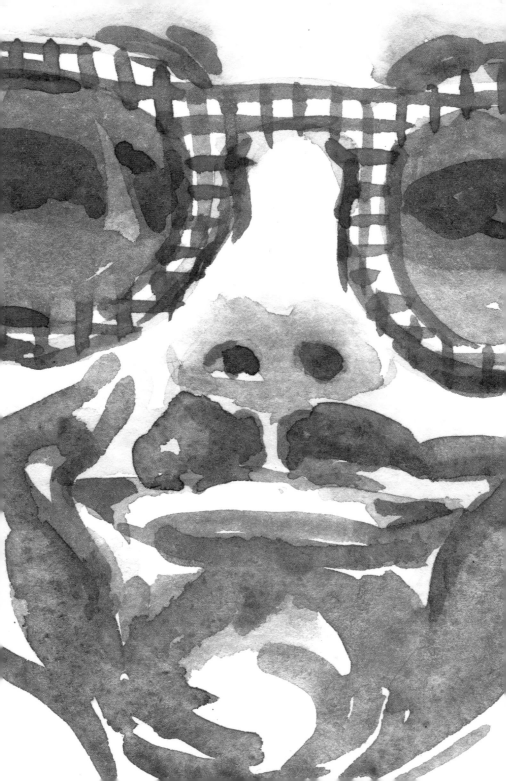

32

Can one mix metals: that is, silver and gold?

Many pieces of jewelry have mixtures of silver and gold in them.

Joyce

I have worn a watch with this combination for years. By and large, if I am wearing gold or silver earrings, the rest of my jewelry such as a necklace or bracelets is gold or silver. My watch remains constant though.

A single item with combined metals makes it effortless.

Nancy

The good news is that many individual pieces of jewelry incorporate silver and gold. David Yurman is a master. Wearing that item gives "permission" to finish with silver or gold or some combination.

Absolutely.

Jay

There are no rules for this kind of thing!

Yes.

Liz

You can mix metals.

No.

Craig

Simple is better. That means one metal or metallic at a time. One at a time, from head to toe.

"There are no rules for this kind of thing!"

33

French women wear scarves. How can I add these to my wardrobe?

Joyce

Buy to enhance facial coloring, collect those you love, and learn a few ways to tie them.

French women have both a history and a knack for collecting and wearing wonderful scarves, especially Hermès and Chanel. Look for beautiful scarves when browsing or traveling. If you see one you love, buy it. I always look for colors that flatter my facial coloring. Learn a few simple scarf "tricks." I know of three. **1.** Fold a square scarf diagonally and tie it around your neck loosely. **2.** Tie a knot in the middle of a square scarf, fold it into a triangle and tie it behind your neck. **3.** Tie a loose knot in the end of a square scarf. Fold it diagonally and thread the opposite corners though the knot. Scarves are never out of fashion, but at times, they are more popular.

Nancy

Practically and simply.

If you are a woman (or man) who finds wearing accessories frivolous or complicated, approach a scarf functionally. If you are attending a wedding, for instance, and the church or reception space is cool, a pashmina shawl can be thrown over the shoulders, adding modesty, style, and warmth simultaneously. A favorite look that is easy to pull off is to take a long oblong scarf and center it at the front of the neck, cross it in the back, and pull the sides to the front. That technique doesn't even require a knot, and can be worn very casually—even with shorts or jeans. Silk scarves are slippery and anchoring them in place can be annoying. Knitted or other woven versions are more compliant. Heavily beaded trim on a silk or velvet evening scarf also can anchor it into place.

Jay

Oversized wraps are a number one choice.

What kind of scarves? Isn't that a cliché now? I dislike when women wear little printed scarves tied tightly at their neck. It looks like they are choking themselves. Oversized wraps are always good in lightweight fabrics. They show off beautiful fabrics and incorporate nice amounts of color and pattern and still don't look garish—just subtle and soft.

Liz

A large shawl, wrapped loosely.

I don't think small scarves do much but look uncomfortable. If you want to add color, pattern, or texture then a larger wrap is nice, just don't wrap it up too closely to your face.

Craig

A number of ways.

Scarves. One of the greatest accessories ever worn—short, long, wide, narrow, printed, solid, bulky, or delicate. Wear them over or under jackets, over the shoulder, around the neck, or tied around your handbag. Be creative and remember you can travel easily with solid, neutral wardrobe pieces and bring out color with a lot of different scarves.

34

What accessories should women have to be ready for most occasions?

Joyce

Basic and simple.

Jewelry, such as hoop earrings and studs (dressy and daytime variety), scarves (square and long), shawls, a simple black and brown belt, a dressy novelty belt, a good day bag, a satin or silk evening bag, shoes in a high heel, low heel, black satin, silver and gold sandal. That's a good start.

Nancy

Depends on personal style.

A simple accessory wardrobe for day may include: leather bag, flats, pumps, gloves, and belt in best neutral, hoop earrings and bangle in best metal, tank watch, pearls and chains of varying lengths, and some scarves. For evening: satin bag, shoes, and stone drop earrings. Those who favor decorative dressing need to pump up all the categories with bigger, more interesting choices.

Jay

Shoes, a statement ring, and Hermès.

Amazing shoes. One disgustingly huge ring and Hermès.

Liz

Shoes and a great bag; the rest is icing.

Shoes. I know this because I am often unprepared. Also, a nice bag. These two things are the most necessary; jewelry and all the rest is just icing. For me personally, I would also say a statement ring is essential.

Craig

Think of a jacket as the base.

A black jacket, scarves for day and night, pearls, jet black and metallic jewelry, a great neutral shoe, and a matching handbag that goes from day to evening.

35

How can I change an outfit that I wear to work into something

New accessories, plus a sophisticated top.

Joyce

I would do several things to change a conservative outfit. Replace "daytime" earrings. Replace a shirt with a jersey or silk top with a low neckline. Carry a small handbag and wear great high heels.

Take off the blouse, pull back the hair, and apply hairspray and red lipstick.

Nancy

This advice works for those who wear a suit to work. Put on some great big earrings, too. Good to go.

Shoes, shoes, shoes.

Jay

Get out of your bad office shoes and rock something chic. Wear a more festive earring to take the suit more evening, and unbutton your jacket to showcase more of whatever. Blouses and shirts pack easily and can be quickly changed after work.

dressier for a party after work?

Shoes. Change your shoes.

Liz

Unbutton your jacket or bring a blouse. Don't worry about jewelry; keep the watch, can be very chic. Change your hair.

Work from a solid-colored dress, or change into an evening jacket.

Craig

Wear a great solid-colored dress, not separates. A blazer-style jacket can easily be changed by adding a sexier or more elegant top for the evening. It's also easy to change jewelry, shoes, and possibly add an evening style belt.

36

Should hosiery match your shoes or your outfit?

Simple works.

Joyce

Wear very simple hosiery. Wear opaque hosiery in the colder months. Wear sheer black hosiery in the winter with dark cocktail attire. In the spring or summer, wear neutral colors.

All of the above.

Nancy

A shoe, leg, and hem all in the same color create a longer, leggier look. Who doesn't want to look long and leggy? Right now, fashion seems to have banned nude hosiery. I'm not sure this is such a good idea. Bare legs are really sexy, but pasty legs (young and old) are not. If you skip stockings, you better have great legs and a good pedicure.

Depends if you want to make a statement or not.

Jay

I didn't even know this is something people think about! If the look is about your shoes (granted, you have good ones) then match your clothes. If it's about the suit, then match the shoes.

Depends on the shoe, I guess.

Liz

If it looks too separate from your outfit, and it's not a good shoe then "yes."

Coordinating an overall look for the outfit is what counts.

Craig

Metallic shoes have become the neutral and the preferred color of hosiery is changing seasonally now.

37

Should hosiery be worn with sandals?

NO!

Joyce
There are some women who always want support. Brands like Spanx have hosiery that controls but comes to just the ankle or a little higher. In general, do not wear hosiery with sandals.

There are no absolute "no's."

Nancy
I've seen some great looks that feature opaque stockings and open-toed shoes in colder months.

Depends on the sandal.

Jay
This isn't a rule that bothers me unless it's a thong that goes between the toes—that would be crazy!

Hmm...

Liz
Could be interesting but usually "no."

No more scandal.

Craig
The most modern look would be to leave the hosiery at home when you are wearing a short dress. It used to be a bit scandalous for women to dress without hosiery, but the rules have definitely been updated.

"It used to be a bit scandalous for women to dress without hosiery, but the rules have definitely been updated."

38

Are shawls still popular? If so what color(s) do you suggest

Joyce

Always, yes.

The basic colors I recommend are black, white, and red. If you find a wonderful shawl in a color that you love, buy that. I have a favorite old piano shawl with long fringe that I have worn for years.

Nancy

Yes.

They are functional, warm, soft, and flattering. Buy one the color of your eyes.

Jay

Yes.

Whatever looks nice against your skin, makes you smile, and you enjoy, is chic. Nothing gypsy though. You can just buy cloth and wrap yourself in it. That is easy, cheap, and custom!

Liz

Yes, especially vintage.

It's always good to have one in a bright color that brings out your natural coloring to wear with simple dresses, but I have several neutral colored shawls that I wear as scarves or hoods. You can always use a piece of fabric as well. I save the extra from hems and often use them as shawl/scarves.

having in your wardrobe?

Shawls are a standard.

Craig

They can be a sexy, covered up alternative to a jacket over a dress or top without sleeves. Keep the allure and learn the many different ways to wear a shawl that can change the look of the outfit. It's an easy add-on when you have basic colors to choose from in your wardrobe such as black, red, and ivory.

39   Are hats passé?

Joyce

Not your mother's hat.

Hats are not as popular today as they were in my mother's era. She used to go religiously to a milliner and have beautiful hats made. She wore them during the day, to luncheons, and even to nightclubs. Today, our lifestyle is different—more casual. Still, there are times when women do wear hats to luncheons, horse races, weddings, holidays, and religious events. I have always loved hats and have enjoyed wearing them.

Nancy

Something so functional can never be passé.

As we write, hats are serving a functional role for sports, for warmth, for bad hair days. They are never passé for British royalty and formal occasions in the U.K.! Certain faces look fantastic framed with a hat and others not so much. One must be comfortable in a decorative hat to wear it without affectation. Hair and hat must work together. Fashion history reveals how hair has often changed to accommodate hat styles.

Jay

Only for the truly chic.

Most people look really affected in hats. Only the truly chic can pull them off. As a generic rule I say "no hats," but some of my best friends always look amazing in hats. They aren't the typical persons, though. You know, the one that worries about hosiery matching shoes!

Liz

If you have the face.

It takes a special face to look comfortable under a hat. If it feels natural, then go for it. Hats are amazing, but I personally can't wear them without anxiety. I have the pleasure of working with several women at the vintage store that can pull off the most ridiculous hats. I think hats are easier as you get older because you have to be sophisticated to pull off something playful without looking ridiculous.

Craig

Only for the occasion.

Leave the hat in the box unless you're on the way to a derby, polo match, or wedding.

40

What are your favorite kinds of accessories and why?

Belts, scarves, and jewelry.

Joyce

I like accessories because they give personality to your appearance and versatility to your clothing. Often, great accessories can define an outfit. They are fun to collect, too.

Jewelry.

Nancy

I love accessories and depend on them extensively for my own personal style. Most pieces in my wardrobe are neutral in color and shape. Interest, for me, comes in the decorative aspects of dressing. I can't get enough of cameos, chokers, hoops, and huge rings. And, most especially, I love the mix. For me, one necklace is not enough. I sometimes combine three or four. I prefer an armload of bangles to one. Jewelry is my thing—more so than shoes, bags, and scarves. As a toddler, I carried around an old green handbag full of junk jewelry. My love for costume jewelry seems instinctive. I don't care about real jewelry. I can't get it big enough to enjoy.

Jay

Just shoes, a smile, and a ring.

Shoes are chic and make plain clothes look great. Shoes first, smile second. A smile is also chic and makes people like you. Also add an amazing ring that screams, "I am on top of it!"

Liz

Really good shoes.

A good shoe empowers you and makes you stand taller and straighter. Since shoes are functional, the more unusual they are and the more amazing the engineering/design is, the more they represent fashionable dressing. Also, rings—your hands are such a statement of whom you are that it's nice to draw attention to them. Find the one that you feel naked without.

Craig

Three favorites.

Belts, scarves, and jewelry.

Organization

"I like my money where I can see it, hanging in my closet."
—**Carrie Bradshaw,** *Sex in the City*

What does an organized closet look like?

Joyce

Neat and tidy.

You're able to quickly find and coordinate very quickly whatever you so desire.

Nancy

Items hanging together by category and color.

I like to separate the pieces of suits; that is, to hang the jackets with other jackets and the skirts/pants with similar items. I think of each separate piece as an item and maximize the ways it can be worn.

Jay

Everything has its place and like items together.

I am still trying to figure this out myself. A few things: matching hangers (anything other than wire), coats and jackets on coat hangers to hold their shape, woven shirts on shirt hangers, shoes not smashed in the laundry basket, pants/skirts hung on pant hangers, not folded over shirt or coat hangers, and sweaters folded on shelves.

The key is visibility.

Liz

I wouldn't really know. I would like to blame this on the fact that I move every three months and I don't really have a closet…sounds good. I can tell you how to organize a suitcase and what I would do if I had a closet. If you want to remember to wear that pair of pants you wore a year ago, you better be able to see them. Don't pile things on top of each other and don't haphazardly layer things on hangers. As I work with limited space, I will hang outfits together, but only if I can see every piece. Give your clothes and your mind some breathing room. Ideally, you want at least 10% of your hanging space to be empty so you can move. Clear out pieces that don't fit or that you won't wear in the current season. Organize by color and by detail. This helps you choose things based on appropriateness and occasion. Color sorting helps you see things that work together and categorizing by detail helps you select for events/weather. When working with very limited shelving space, you can increase visibility by rolling. Fold neatly, and then roll.

Craig

Organized by season, category, or color.

Oops, and size…if it's always changing.

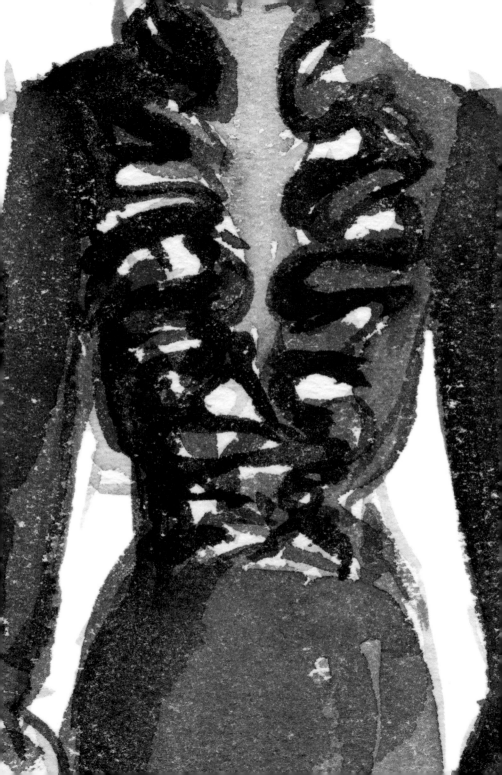

Take everything out of the closet.

Joyce

Go through your clothes one item at a time. Sort out what you do not wear. Return to your closet the things you do wear in an orderly manner. Group clothes into categories; for example, slacks, skirts, suits, blouses, dresses, novelty jackets, and evening clothes. Within the categories, group color families. On shelves, place handbags and/or shoes. Accessories such as evening bags can be stored in drawers or a plastic container.

Twice yearly inventory.

Nancy

All items come out of the closet and are considered for the season, fit, purpose, etc. If the garment is unwearable in any way (including a need to be ironed or repaired), retire it until it's ready to wear. Then, wearable items return to the closet again arranged by silhouette and by color. I use the color method I learned in retailing: white, yellow, green, blue, red, lavender, brown, and then follow with black.

Decipher the problem.

Jay

Do you want better access to certain items? Are your shoes the issue? Can you not find room for coats? Measure the space you have

Mine is such a mess.

for storage. Also, think vertically to take full advantage of total space. Go to any home store (Target; Bed, Bath and Beyond; The Container Store, etc.). Find potential items that suit your needs. Measure them. Go back to your closet. Mark out the system so the items that need to be there fit into the space.

Liz

Hang items for best visibility.

If room does not allow you to hang everything, hang the items that need to be hung to stay in good condition. Categorize by garment type: dresses, pants, shirts, etc. Within those categories, hang by color: white, cream, nude, pink, red, etc. Within color, hang by detail: strapless, sleeveless, short-sleeved, long-sleeved, etc. When folding, stack based on size, with the largest on the bottom. This way, you increase visibility. If room doesn't allow folding and stacking, roll instead. You would be surprised how much more room there is when garments are rolled.

Craig

Buy organizers and follow the color/ category rule.

Keep things you want to wear within sight and always put things immediately back into place after wearing.

43

How often should you give your closet a thorough cleaning?

Joyce

Twice a year as the seasons change.

Remove the clothes you will not be wearing and store them in another closet, basement, storage boxes or even at the dry cleaners. Some dry cleaners even offer free storage. Of course, if you lead a more hectic life, your closets may get messy more often.

Nancy

At the beginning and end of summer.

I wear the same clothing during the autumn, winter, and spring for the most part. Only when it gets really hot or cold do I feel the need for a closet redo.

Jay

Yearly.

If you're selective in your buying, there is no real need to consistently rid yourself of things or seriously redo your closet. If you have to retire things that are virtually falling apart, hopefully it is because you've "worn the items to death" out of sheer love. If not, and your clothing is showing early wear, look at what kinds of items you are purchasing and how you are taking care of them.

Every three months.

Liz
It's better to do small amounts more frequently.

Every season.

Craig
To keep it clean and up-to-date.

44

How do you store scarves neatly?

Scarves can be stored a number of ways.

Joyce

You can fold them and store in drawers. You can hang them on skirt hangers or you can hang them on special scarf hangers. These hangers have a variety of holes in solid plastic. You just thread the scarves through the holes. Specialty organizing stores usually sell them.

I simply fold them.

Nancy

In squares then stack, again by color.

Fold and roll.

Jay

Fold silk scarves and roll wool ones.

On hangers.

Liz

Hang them on stacked pant hangers or buy the hangers with holes at the top that allow you to slip the scarf through.

Rings.

Craig

Buy rings at the hardware store. Put the rings on a hanger and slip the scarves through the rings.

"I simply fold them."

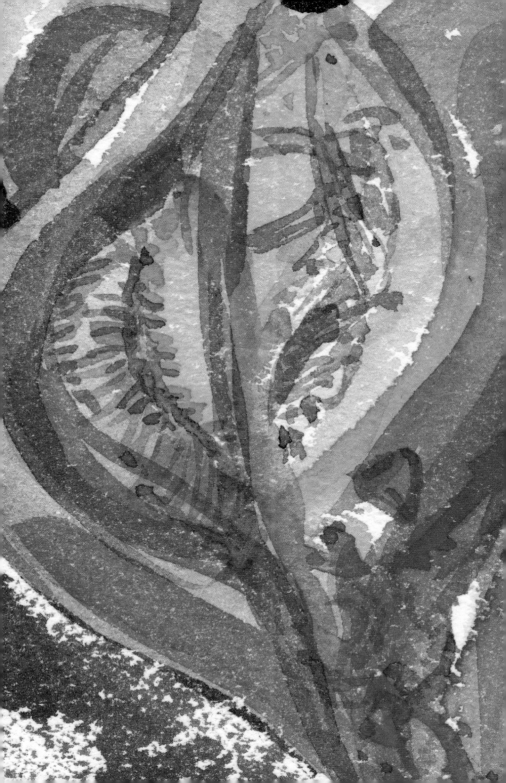

45

Is there a way to organize handbags? Belts?

Joyce

By color and season for bags; racks for belts.

Handbags often come with soft bags for storage purposes. If your closet has space, store by color on a shelf. Handbags have a tendency to fall over. Shelf dividers are available that will eliminate this. Keep the out-of-season bags separate. Group together and store in another place. Purchase a belt rack. Some racks will hang on doors; others function like a hanger and fit right in the closet among the clothes.

Nancy

Consider clear, pocketed hanging accessory bags.

I have seen beautiful closets mostly in magazines where shelving is appropriate and expansive enough to display handbags, again by type and by color. I have seen other examples of plastic storage bins for bags and trays or hanging rings for belts. My handbags are simply placed on a shelf, by type—daytime separate from evening. My smaller belts are rolled and placed in a hanging accessory bag that has multiple clear pockets. I use the same tool for storing earrings, bracelets, necklaces, brooches, etc. Larger belts are rolled and placed on a shelf by color.

Even on a bookshelf.

Jay

By color and/or material. Hang belts on a belt hanger and place bags in a row on your shelf. If it's a beautiful bag, consider placing it on a bookshelf. If you don't have a great bag, consider buying yourself one that you would display.

Divided boxes for handbags and belt racks for belts.

Liz

If you don't have a rack, roll your belts and place them in a shallow drawer.

Belts are easily hung on hooks on the back of the door.

Craig

Bags are tricky. Consider putting small bags inside of large ones.

46

How do you suggest storing shoes?

A number of ways.

Joyce

If you have room, place shoes in plastic boxes and label. Store on shelves. Group by classification such as heels, flats, dressy, casual. Shoes can also be stored on the floor of the closet on one of the many rack styles available. If space is a problem, investigate storage organizers that fit on the backs of doors. Keep shoes polished and heeled at all times.

I personally don't like shoeboxes.

Nancy

I line shoes up (without protection) on shelves by color, heel height, and type. I have a friend who takes Polaroids of all of her shoes and attaches the photo to the original shoebox. She buys really expensive shoes, though.

Open shoe boxes lined up on shelves or in plastic shoe boxes with a photograph of the shoe outside.

Jay

This will protect your shoes from dirt, look nice on the shelf, and you can see what you own. Put like items together; that is, boots with boots, pumps with pumps, and sandals with sandals. This will also show you if you're buying too much of the same thing. I also recommend using cedar shoe trees. Sand them every year as the cedar is only effective if it's refreshed. Unrefreshed cedar will not absorb moisture. I loathe shoes stored in baggies or in racks on the back of doors. Very unattractive!

Liz

Shoes are easily ruined and forgotten.

Store shoes in good condition, either in a shoe bag with a label or a box with the description. I prefer to stuff the shoes with tissue paper and put them in a bag. This method takes less room and I can hang the bag if I don't have enough shelf space.

Craig

In clear shoe boxes.

Put the most frequently worn near the front.

Should sweaters be folded or hung?

Joyce

Folded to prevent stretching.

Often they are placed in plastic zip storage bags, too. This protects them against moths.

Nancy

Hang for practicality and visibility, but not for care.

We all know that folding prevents stretching, but since I own so many black garments, folding isn't practical. I have to hang my sweaters so that I can see the details.

Jay

Folded.

Absolutely should never be hung. If the shoulders of your sweater get stretched out, use a hot iron and apply heavy steam to the yarn (without directly touching the iron to the sweater). Pat with your hand to bring the yarn back to life.

Liz

Ideally, folded.

Some are tightly woven enough to hang on a foam hanger so that you can see them. Again, roll for more room.

Craig

Folded.

You don't have to have them blocked, if you fold.

What types of hangers do you suggest?

Joyce

Anything but wire.

There are many types to choose from. It is nice to have all hangers match in color or type. Use a heavy plastic hanger for blouses, jackets, and dresses. Pants should be hung individually on specific pant hangers. Ideally, hang suits on hangers that have pant or skirt hangers included with the jacket hanger.

Nancy

I am not particular about hangers, and many of the large wooden ones simply take up too much space.

I like flat velveteen hangers that don't take up too much room and prevent the garments from slipping.

Jay

Wood.

If you don't want to spend money on wood, then get white plastic. If you are using proper pant/skirt hangers, then please use suede or cloth pads to protect the fabric from the grip of the hanger. There is nothing worse than seeing pants or skirts wrecked by hangers without pads—especially leather, suede, velvet, and corduroy (basically anything delicate with a nap to it).

Liz

Black, skinny velvet hangers.

They aren't slippery and they don't take any extra room. Obviously, no wire hangers (I hope).

Craig

With padding or foam.

Hangers with padding or foam for delicate clothing. Coat hangers for jackets and clips for pants/bottom.

What do you do with out of season clothing?

Joyce

Remove out of season clothing from your closet.

This frees up room in the closet which enable clothes to "breathe." Store clothes wherever you can—in another closet, suitcases, cartons, the basement or at the drycleaner.

Nancy

At the dry cleaners.

They charge nothing to store, only to clean.

Jay

I live in NY, so there's not much room for out-of-season storage.

With appropriate space, I may separate warm from cold weather clothing, and put year-round items in between. Since I have a small closet, I keep shoes at the bottom. I keep all of my pants together (wool to linen) and have them lined up by type (pleated, pinstriped, corduroy, denim). Coats together (on heavy wooden coat hangers), jackets together (nicer ones in cloth garment bags and on nice wooden jacket hangers); and shirts together by color (on white plastic hangers). I have sweaters folded on the top shelf. I'm tall so it's easy for me to access the top shelf. If you're not, buy a small step ladder that can be stored flat against the wall. If you have more money and tall ceilings, get one of those amazing library ladders that travel the length of your closet on a track. Make sure to use the full height of your closets.

Rice bags.

Liz

They are strong, a lot more attractive than garbage bags and still provide more space than boxes. When storing, I categorize more by when I expect to wear the items next than what type of garment it is. When the season is over, I can retrieve the next season's choices as I need them.

Craig

Vacuum sealed bags.

Store in vacuum sealed bags with dryer sheets for freshness.

50

If something has not been worn in a year should it be given away?

There are no rules.

Joyce

You may want to retire the item and bring it back at a future date. Do so and do not feel one bit guilty.

Not necessarily.

Nancy

I would remove it from the closet, but store it if it's special or beautiful in any way.

"Absolutely not" is the quick answer, but...

Jay

If it's a tee shirt that you bought for $5.00 because it was $5.00, give it away if you haven't worn it, and shame on you. If it's something you love, but just don't wear it all the time, hold onto it. If it's something that you don't wear, but it has sentimental value to you, keep it. If it's something you don't wear because you can't fit into it, get rid of it. Either lose the weight or get rid of it and stop kidding yourself. Don't torture yourself by looking at it. "Skinny" jeans are not motivation. Having clothes you love and want to wear is motivation. If it's something you don't wear, but are hoping will come back in style, get rid of it. There is no use in holding on to something that has no value in your current life. And chances are that by the time it comes back in "style," you will already have "rocked" that style and won't want to relive it ever again.

What is the reason?

Liz

If it is not in the best condition, then "yes," give it away. If it's not good quality, give it away. Many of my favorite pieces I've had for years, but I wear them regularly. Be honest. Don't think things that are expensive are valuable. Wearing is what creates value. If you can't bear to give a "label" away, sell it on eBay or in a consignment shop

If it doesn't fit, give it away.

Craig

If it is a timeless piece and it stills looks fresh on you and fits properly, hold onto it for one more year, and see if you revive it.

Budget

"It's not money that makes you well dressed, it's understanding."
—Christian Dior

51

Do you believe buying "on sale" is a good idea?

Joyce

Buying smart is the best idea.

If you have a well thought-out wardrobe and know your needs, buying on sale is great. If you are buying just because it is a bargain and you have no idea how you will use the item in your wardrobe, buying on sale is dangerous. This will lead to having a "closet full of clothes and nothing to wear."

Nancy

Cautious buying "on sale" is an excellent idea.

A garment's value is based on a "cost per wearing" ratio. Today, I am wearing an expensive Donna Karan sweater that I bought at full price. I have had it for fifteen years and have worn it hundreds of times. This costly garment truly is a "bargain," when compared to some items that I have bought on sale. The dress that was marked down from $400 to $50 is really expensive if it's only worn a few times.

Jay

I love sales.

But, buying "on sale" isn't a good idea if you see something you love, wait for the markdown and then it's gone. The other times sales are not a good idea is when you convince yourself to buy something because it is on sale and then you never wear it. You should save all those mistakes so you can afford your Hermès bag and big diamonds—seriously.

**Buying is good
when you love
something, on
sale or not.**

Liz

If you see an item at full price and you can't justify buying it, wait. But, if you see an item that you really love, buy it immediately. It evens out because I know that if I get the one piece I really want, I won't want anything else for a while. The worth of any item in terms of its actual material value can be very similar or different than its perceived value, which can also be very different from personal value. I don't believe in only shopping the sale section. You can't justify buying things you like but don't love. You have to feel satisfied and fulfilled after a purchase otherwise you will just keep buying.

**Saving money is
always a good
idea, but not
always possible.**

Craig

If you need something right away and it is on sale, buy it. However, if you need something specific in size, color, and style, buy it when you first see it. It may not be available if you wait for a sale day.

52

Can you help me avoid costly mistakes when purchasing fashion?

Be cautious of sales, moods, and unrelated color choices.

Joyce

When you find a sale, only buy what works with your existing wardrobe. Avoid a random sale item. Buy complete outfits that are on sale. When building a wardrobe, stick to one basic color at first, then enhance with special unique items after the basics are covered. Do not buy when you are unhappy. One tends to spend more at this time. Watch binge buying.

Evaluate, listen, think.

Nancy

Try things on. Shop with a trusted sales associate. Do not buy at the last minute for special occasions. Avoid impulse buying.

Shop with me!

Jay

Otherwise—no. Advice I would give would seem contradictory unless I knew each individual reading these words.

One tip.

Liz
Don't buy something unless you want to wear it at that very moment.

The golden rule—buy classic and timeless.

Craig
The hottest item of the season is often a one-season deal that is the most expensive. First, buy what you love and secondly, buy what you like. Pass on anything you question that you may not want in your closet next month!

53

What is your opinion regarding shopping online or by catalog?

Joyce

Beware of online and catalog buying.

You must realize that the items online as well as in catalogs don't always photograph the same color and texture as those you will receive. The same applies to sizing. You may order the size you think you wear and the cut of these items may not be the same. If you are willing to take a chance and know you may have some returns, buying online can often provide some unique items not found in stores.

Nancy

I love buying online, but be careful.

Shopping online is wonderful, especially for items that don't need to "fit," or if one is a fairly easy fit. Additionally, persons who can read and understand fabrics will have more luck. Shopping online or by category opens up the shopping world for those of us who live in cities without a wide range of shopping opportunities. Because I study fashion and know the lines that suit me, fit me, and are known for quality, I don't always have to try the item on or touch it to know that it will suit me.

Jay

Would NEVER do it.

How are you supposed to buy something without trying it on? I don't even buy things in thrift stores without trying them on. I wouldn't buy something unless I touched it and saw its true color and fabric. This is so confusing to me and I couldn't even justify it because of convenience. I don't buy books or music online either. Never have.

Liz

Impossible.

I have a friend in the fashion industry, living in NYC, who only buys online. I never buy anything that I can't touch. I need to feel it and see the color and almost always try it on, unless it's a duplicate of something I already have. But, even then, sometimes...neurotic. But, I realize that some people see clothes better on someone else. This particular friend of mine has amazing style and will literally go through magazines and tear out what she wants to wear and somehow locates it online. She is perfectly satisfied judging a garment for herself by the way it looks on someone else, and she doesn't try things on. Even if I like what looks good on a hanger or in a picture, I still need to try it on. I might like it better on me if I wear it upside down.

Craig

Great for accessories.

They are often less expensive and easy to purchase. Sized items are more difficult and may be a hassle to return. Check out the site and the return policies before you buy anything.

How does one stay current on a budget?

Joyce

Look carefully and evaluate.

At the beginning of each season, there are numerous magazines that forecast the upcoming trends. Color, accessories, jackets, shoes, skirt length, pant styles are all discussed at this time. Take your time and visit the stores in your area. What is your lifestyle? Will these items fit in with the needs of your life? Are these trends appropriate for your age or your figure? Select one or two of these to coordinate with your existing clothes. Often a strong trend is very expensive at its onset, but will be available at a less costly price a month or so after the trend first appears. I do not recommend spending a great deal on a strong trend that will be out the following season.

Nancy

Do some basic research and pick a few key items.

There is good information available to us from so many sources. We can see major runway shows online as they occur in Paris, New York, or Milan. Read a condensed version of key fashion trends by a fashion editor you admire. Pick a few really new fashion items and incorporate those items into your basic wardrobe. Accessories can be a less costly way to look "of the moment."

Jay

Discover the person you are on the inside and let your clothing be an extension of yourself.

Don't buy to stay current. Don't buy impulsively. Obtain something you really want and then wear it "to death" because of your guilt (that is what works for me!). Six months later, I realize how happy I am to wear and own this thing that I still love so much.

Liz

Waistline is key.

One easy thing to do is simply to pay attention to where the waistline is trend-wise. This is the most obvious proportion and easiest to adjust. You can use belts or layers to achieve the proportion that makes you feel "current" and hopefully comfortable. I can't say enough, however, about buying what you love. It will always feel right.

Craig

Again, there's a golden rule.

It's easy to stay current and within a budget if you buy classic and timeless items such as a great jacket, dress, or suit that can be updated with a belt, shoes, accessorizes in new colors, and scarves.

55

How much of my budget should I allocate for clothes,

Joyce

Your lifestyle determines your needs.

This will obviously depend on the total amount of money that you spend on clothes per year. Personally, in September, I think about the clothes I will need the following year. When I worked, I usually liked to buy one pantsuit, one skirt suit, a dressy outfit, and a new pair of black heels and brown heels. About every two years, I purchased a new coat. I would add sweaters and accessories as the need arose. Now that I am not working, I have different needs. I buy several pairs of slacks, a cardigan sweater and a slip over, flat shoes, a dressy dress and a pantsuit. Again, I add sweaters, blouses, accessories and shoes as I need them. I need more casual clothes now.

Nancy

A matter of resources, lifestyle, and preferences.

I heard many years ago that the average American spends $3,000 a year on clothing and accessories. That makes me above average. Many, I know, consider that figure high. Clothing is a priority for me. I have spent much of my life in fashion. For others, it is not so important. Casual lifestyles require less. It's personal. I could easily spend 100% of my clothing budget on accessories. They are my priority.

shoes and accessories?

Jay

Depends on what your priorities are.

If you want a small apartment, no car, and Hermès then plan to spend a lot on your wardrobe! If you want a mansion, Mercedes, and a Coach bag, you'll obviously need less. Those of us who love fashion may decide against the week in the Bahamas so that we can look the way we want to look every day of the year. There are so many different people, tastes, lifestyles, unforeseen financial situations, etc. to accurately suggest a universal percentage.

Liz

Not sure yet.

As a young student who doesn't make much, I don't really have the privilege of budgeting but I understand giving up one thing for another.

Craig

Keep the largest budget for neutral basics.

If you wear mostly black, invest more on your basics in black and less on a seasonal color or trend items. Your clothes should make the largest percentage of a budget followed by shoes and then accessories.

56

Do you think estimating how much a yearly wardrobe will cost and

Your bank account determines.

Joyce

I think estimating a yearly budget for clothes is a fascinating idea. I know a very fashion savvy person who does this very well. She decides on a yearly clothing budget and sticks to it. If she wants to spend a considerable amount on one item, such as a belt, she does and knows there will be less later for something else. She is okay with this. I am not that disciplined. I have a general idea regarding what I need, but I may see something I can use and not want the limitations of budget. If a budget plan appeals to you, try it for six months and see how you manage.

Who can argue with the wisdom of a budget?

Nancy

That being said, I can never stay on one.

sticking to that amount is a good idea?

Who buys a wardrobe yearly?

Jay

Buy what you love when you see it, and you will wear it for a very long time. Move around finances, if necessary. Cook and eat at home and buy the bag you love. Never buy a yearly (or seasonal) wardrobe at once. The clothing won't sustain your interest, need, or occasion.

No.

Liz

Don't think of a wardrobe as "yearly."

Make a plan and work the plan.

Craig

Sticking to a budget will alleviate angst and stress. There will always be a new great dress. It's endless.

When one is on a budget what are the best months to buy

Joyce

Plan ahead. Designers and manufacturers are usually six months ahead of a season. That means a store buyer goes to market in September/October and buys spring. Spring is delivered in February/March. Fall clothes are delivered in August/September. About six weeks after delivery, the first markdowns are taken. I always think the best clothes of the season are delivered the earliest. As you see something begin to arrive in the store, you may check back about six weeks after its receipt to anticipate its markdown. At the end of the selling season, for instance, after the Fourth of July or Christmas, markdowns are wonderful.

Nancy

Stay vigilant. Markdowns are occurring earlier and earlier in a season. Traditionally, swimsuits were marked down after the Fourth of July. Now, there is a price break in May or early June. I would say to really watch your favorite stores to see when there are special sales or major price breaks. Ask your sales associate to notify you when price breaks or when there is a temporary reduction of prices for special events.

spring clothes; autumn clothes?

To be safe, buy what you love as soon as you see it.

Jay

You won't be tempted to buy the great deal on a winter coat, because you're happy with your beloved winter coat. For instance, I wanted a new Jil Sander coat. I waited for the 50% markdown, my size was gone. Dreams shattered. That being said, there are great sales periods. Post Thanksgiving, usually 30% off; post Christmas, sometimes 75% off.

Seasonal sale shopping is not important.

Liz

I wear the same wardrobe year-round. For special values, after the Fourth of July and after the 1st of the year, savings seem greatest.

Call your favorite store and ask the sales people.

Craig

Every store runs sales as needed to reduce inventory and give consumers an incentive to show up. But, times are changing rapidly, and the best advice is to meet a salesperson you trust and let them call you when you want to start shopping a sale. Many stores offer pre-sale purchases, and then you get the first pick of sale merchandise!

58

On what items do you think one should spend the most money?

Joyce

Shoes, handbags, a dress coat, a black suit.

These often will define your look. They will be the items you wear most frequently. If you amortize them. You will see that in the end they will not be the most costly.

Nancy

Items that will be life-changing because they will last forever, simplify your life, or give you a special sense of beauty or personal value.

There are certain pieces that you will rely on. We call them "workhorses," because you constantly reach for them, you feel comfortable, and look good in them. They often can pull together random items that previously hung idle in the closet. A smart new item will give value to the old. A very expensive black cashmere skirt that fits and anchors a number of other pieces may prove priceless. I bought a pair of leggings for $60.00 about fifteen years ago. The price at the time seemed outrageous. I have them on now. They are so comfortable. They haven't worn out. I could wear them to a party and get away with it. There's an old movie called *Mrs. 'Arris Goes to Paris*. Angela Lansbury "gives it all up" for a Dior gown. It's transformative. To have that kind of relationship with a piece of clothing would be special!

The things you wear everyday— shoes, double-faced cashmere, etc.

Jay

Those items are what I spend money on. Wise choices for others may be a coat, a killer dress, shoes, a bag—the rest you can skimp on.

A good coat.

Liz

It's an awful feeling to have to cover up an amazing dress with a bad coat...embarrassing. I've gotten sick because of this.

Timeless, classic investment pieces.

Craig

A great versatile black dress, a black jacket, and a white blouse—timeless, classic and worth the investment.

59

Is it better to buy everything for a season at once and preplan how

I would say it is harder to buy everything for a season at once.

Joyce

However, I know a lady who does just this. She has a budget of around $2,500 and she makes an appointment with a personal shopper and purchases all of the things she wants for that season. She is not a shopper and just wants it done. She has done this for years and religiously comes in twice a year to do this. In general, this is hard because the chance of your actually finding everything you want during one visit is almost impossible. I would suggest buying one or two complete outfits and adding to your wardrobe periodically.

It depends on your attitude toward shopping and your ability to do it well.

Nancy

If you hate to shop and have the need to look great, do it all at once working with a fashion professional to focus your purchases and perfect your look. If you like to shop or buy things when you travel, your method is quite different.

much to spend at this time or buy smaller amounts continually?

Jay

No.

Smaller amounts continually—always.

Liz

No.

Smaller amounts—don't force anything.

Craig

Look at your calendar of events, work needs, and vacation time— see what you need and when.

If you can, buy your key items at one time and buy accessories throughout the year. You keep a fresh look and feel up-to-date with your wardrobe.

I am thinking of selling some of my clothes at a resale shop.

Joyce

Yes.

Selling clothes you no longer want will generate money to buy more current items. I am familiar with two resale shops. If you do this, the shop will take 40% and you get 60% of the sale price. Usually, they have a set number of weeks the items are on sale and then mark them down. Remember, the price the store designates may surprise you. It could seem quite low to you. Some charitable outlets sell your clothes and give you a tax deduction. You may find this a better way to go.

Nancy

Yes, or donate.

Although the return is rarely what you think your clothing is worth, it's a smart way to generate "guilt-free" income for new purchases. Charitable donations are important too.

Is this a good idea?

Be gracious, keep what you love, and donate the rest.

Jay

There are some options though. Sometimes you have lost interest in a still valuable item— give that to a friend. It's not a "hand-me-down," just an "I don't want this item to leave my life" gesture. A friend of mine just went to a "clothes swap." For some reason, it seems one is always giving the good stuff and getting the old Gap t-shirt in return.

If it was always bad, don't kid yourself... no one wants it.

Liz

Labels won't even get you money these days so I would suggest donating. If it is something amazing that maybe doesn't fit you, but you want it to have a good home and it has value to you, then sell it to a high-end resale shop.

Could be fun.

Craig

If you have the time to manage your consignment items, it's a great way to get a few extra dollars for fun. Plan to donate items if they don't sell, though.

Personal Shopper

"You can have anything you want in life if you dress for it."
—Edith Head

What is a personal shopper?

Joyce

A definition.

A personal shopper is someone who has fashion experience and is employed to assist customers within a fashion store with their purchases.

Nancy

Quite simply, a personal shopper is one who does retail legwork for another who is less interested in shopping, less talented in wardrobe management, or too busy to shop for his/her wardrobe and other necessities or desires.

A personal shopper may be employed by a store or self-employed. A good personal shopper can simplify life tremendously by editing selections that best fit the client's style and needs. With the help of a seasoned personal shopper, one can look impeccable without ever entering a store or a computer site dedicated to shopping. Most people now seem to understand the need for a wedding planner—someone who ensures the impeccable execution of details. That is the same thing a personal shopper does. If the shopper is employed by a store, the service is usually complimentary. Younger people may not understand why one needs a personal shopper, yet they relate to fashion stylists. A personal shopper may seem too commercial. The truth is that a good personal shopper may be employed by a store, yet completely loyal to a client.

The term personal shopper does not resonate with my generation.

Jay

A personal shopper may be a gay friend or a girlfriend. It may be someone who has great (or moderate) taste and is employed at a department store. It is probably all of these things and more.

I like the idea of a stylist, not a shopper.

Liz

Some personal shoppers may not know you personally and may try to sell you things because of their affiliation with a retailer. If you need help getting dressed, perhaps for something big, get a creative stylist who will give you a lot of options and customize the looks to you.

A personal shopper will help you define your style, keep you up-to-date, prepared, and act as your personal stylist.

Craig

They can keep you informed when new merchandise has arrived or goes on sale. They are also good at locating specific, hard-to-find items that would work for you personally.

62

Every time I go into a store where there is a personal shopper,

Joyce

No.

Use them when the occasion fits your needs. If you use a personal shopper in a particular store, you do not need to use them every time you are in that store.

Nancy

Of course not.

I might add, though, that if there is a personal shopping service, it is usually housed in a very nice area within the store. Often the site of the service is very attractively arranged and stocked with snacks and beverages. The fitting rooms are larger, a tailor responds quickly for alteration needs, shipping can be expedited, etc. If the client wants to walk the store alone, he/she can do so and have the items sent back to the service site to enjoy the enhanced amenities.

Jay

I am not comfortable with the term "shopper," and am often wary about retail associates.

I worry that a shopper will not have sensitivity to the individual, but will be primarily interested in meeting sales goals. I have the same worry about salespersons, though. Once at Barney's, a lady approached me and asked for an honest opinion (although she was with a sales associate). Clearly, I was game. She asked, "Do you like this skirt on me?" I told her honestly that it made her look hippy. She said to her salesperson, "See!" I asked her if it was Alaïa and explained that the skirt had great

do I need to use them?

movement in the back, but was meant for someone who was VERY slim from front to back. All the movement was coming from the wrong place. The salesperson seemed more concerned about selling the $2,300 skirt than making her client look good. I knew that the cut of a Narciso Rodriguez skirt would flatter the client, and suggested it to her as an alternative. If the sales associate had really known fashion and cared about the customer, she could have both secured a sale and a long-term client while making the world a more beautiful place.

Liz

Of course not.

All sales people should be able to help suggest items to you. Hopefully, reliable retailers only employ associates with taste, integrity, and interest in the individual shopper. Remember, the store has already edited its merchandise in the way it believes conforms to the taste of its clients.

Craig

They should respect your wishes at all times.

They are there to assist you. If you tell them you enjoy shopping alone, they should oblige. If you feel pressure, you should find another personal shopper.

63

Do you think department store fashion consultants or personal

Joyce

Yes—these professionals can definitely simplify your life.

Today, you hire specialists for many segments of your life such as interior design, gardening, entertaining and so forth. Personal shoppers can edit for you and save you an immense amount of time with your shopping and gift needs. We are all so busy these days.

Nancy

Yes, I think they can be of immense value for many reasons.

Certain persons lack interest or the talent for putting together their own wardrobes or lack the time for shopping for themselves and for gifts. A personal shopper is like any other professional who offers a service. I personally am not talented in interior design. I hire a professional whose choices reflect my own (because we communicate well) and who can make my home look beautiful. A talented personal shopper will alert a client when new styles arrive that will complement a client's wardrobe, when certain items go on sale, etc. A personal shopper can do the research to identify the right item for important, specific occasions, and simply be on the lookout for smart new selections.

shoppers are of value? If so, why?

Jay

No.

Personal shoppers may add unique, individual advantages, but I personally encourage each individual to become confident in shopping for and expressing his/her unique style.

Liz

No.

Unless you have no time and call ahead to have them pull things for you or you have a very specific event. I see value in a personal shopper as a time-saving tool but not as a service you rely on to choose your wardrobe. Look for the confidence and inspiration to find your own style.

Craig

They are of great value and it is a free service that can save you time and give you great advice.

They can keep your wardrobe up to date, maintain your budget, and keep you informed of store events that may be of interest. They can also help when you need a gift and/or don't have time to shop for yourself.

How do you find a personal shopper?

Joyce

Simply call
and inquire.

Larger fashion stores have this service.

Nancy

Check to see if
your favorite store
employs personal
shoppers.

Usually if the store has this service, there are several shoppers on site. Interview them to see if you are comfortable with their personalities and if you admire their own personal style. Work with them once and see if you feel your needs are met and if your life seems easier because of their services.

Jay

Consider shopping
with your gay son
or a friend you trust
a lot.

Never pay someone to help you (unless you have an Oscar appearance and average taste). Be your own personal shopper by trusting your intuition. If you look in the mirror and think you look bad, or if you're not sure if you look good, take a pass. If you can't trust your intuition, hire a therapist.

Liz

Trust yourself.

If you really need help for something specific and are feeling overwhelmed, get a stylist or call an amazing company. One I am familiar with is the Albright Fashion Library. The stylists there will make sure you leave with a head-to-toe look, feeling luxurious, comfortable, and self-aware. You should always feel like yourself no matter what you are wearing.

Craig

You can find personal shoppers who will work for you as an independent service and are not tied to one specific retailer.

You will pay this type of personal shopper directly. For complimentary personal shopping services, just call a store and see if the store offers the service.

Do you recommend shopping with a friend or alone?

Joyce

I personally shop alone.

I am a very decisive shopper. I like an item or I don't. I have a mission, generally, when I shop. I do not like browsing around all day. If I am on vacation, it is another story. If, however, you are unsure of yourself, take someone along whom you trust to make decisions about style. In the end you are wearing and paying for the item. You are the one who needs to be satisfied.

Nancy

I know my own style, needs, preference, and budget well enough that I don't require a friend's assistance.

I have used a personal shopping service, however, when I need some help with a selection, when I'm strapped for time, or when I have no inclination to go shopping. Some people probably should not be without a personal shopper, just as I should not be without an interior designer. Friends are not necessarily fashion experts, but an objective eye may open our minds to new possibilities.

Jay

I like shopping alone and trust only myself.

I select according to personal preference and come from a place of confidence.

I like shopping alone.

Liz

I trust myself and I hate coming out of the dressing room to show people how I look. Not even my most stylish friends can convince me to buy something. On the other hand, they may be able to convince me NOT to buy something as long as their argument isn't that it is "ugly." I tend to like the unusual thing that others perceive as "ugly." It's all how you wear your clothing. Sometimes I like to throw people off and while I'm young and healthy, I can get away with it...right?

Shopping with a friend who gives you good advice is great.

Craig

If they compete with you, it can be costly.

Can I bring some of my own things to a personal shopper and have

Joyce

Rarely is this successful.

It is better to start anew. Once in a while you could add a newer cut pant with an older classic jacket. Here you should rely on a professional's opinion.

Nancy

Possibly.

If you have an item in your closet that you love, but find you are not wearing it, by all means bring it into the store to get some advice about how to pull it into your working wardrobe.

Jay

I assume so.

Probably.

him/her add items to update the look?

Liz

You could.

At least this would show that you know what you're looking for and have some idea of your personal style.

Craig

Absolutely.

Every personal shopper knows you have clothes in your closet already.

Are there consultants who make "house calls" to do a closer analysis

Joyce

Often this is not productive for the store, the sales person or the client.

I remember doing a closet analysis when I first started in the business many years ago. The client challenged me about each item I told her to eliminate. She would say things like, "Well, maybe I might wear it when I visit my mother-in-law." etc. Finally, I said gently, "Why don't you go downstairs and have some coffee? I will put everything on the bed that you should give away. When I leave, you can just put it all back in your closet."

Nancy

I have heard a number of people say that they would love this service.

But, I would not be too comfortable using it. It's so personal and, for me, an intimate space. But, certain persons and/or retailers provide the service.

Jay

I would be wary of this.

So many would-be fashion experts go on about "good taste," and imagine theirs is better than yours. Not necessarily true.

# of your wardrobe?

Yes.

Liz

But it would be more fun to go on a reality show for kicks.

You can hire a stylist or a person that specializes in organization.

Craig

A stylist can coordinate clothes you already own into new looks and help you achieve a new style if you wish.

How often do you recommend visiting a personal shopper?

Joyce

Twice a year.

I would suggest visiting a personal shopper at least twice a year when the seasons change and the new receipts arrive in the store. Many customers shop more regularly depending on their lifestyle needs.

Nancy

As needed.

Especially when you are really short on time.

Jay

Never.

I simply am uncomfortable with the idea.

Liz

Not for me.

I would not rely on a personal shopper to help me dress.

Craig

Often.

At least one or two times each season.

"I would suggest visiting a personal shopper at least twice a year when the seasons change and the new receipts arrive in the store."

Will a personal shopper help with holiday gifts, anniversary gifts?

Joyce

Yes, usually multi-purpose.

A good personal shopper will help you in any way he/she can. They will know your lifestyle and your needs and will be happy to make suggestions for gifts.

Nancy

Personal shoppers want to manage the whole range of shopping experiences for their clients.

Good personal shoppers, however, never pressure their clients to buy more than they need or to purchase only from them. The relationship with a personal shopper should be one that simplifies one's life tremendously. If there is pressure involved, you're working with the wrong personal shopper.

Jay

Hope not.

Persons should choose their own gifts for others.

**Gifts should
come naturally
and be purchased
by the"giver."**

Liz

I understand this thought, though. Maybe you
hardly know your niece and don't know what
would look good on her. If that is the case,
I would suggest not buying her something
personal for her wardrobe. Gift with money,
or something inspirational, like a book.

Yes.

Craig

They will help you buy anything, including
personal needs.

70

I am very busy with my current job. I would love to be on an automatic

Joyce

Yes, thanks to new technology.

With computer systems in many stores, you can ask your personal shopper to put you on an automatic replenishment system for almost everything you desire.

Nancy

Sophisticated computer systems and record keeping devices to fulfill clients' regular needs are a given.

Simply by working with your shopper or other retail associate, you can set up a system whereby you are regularly charged for an item that needs to be replenished. It arrives at your door at the precise time that you are out of foundation, hosiery, or perfume—whatever the item is that you regularly require. It's like auto-refill at your pharmacy! This service is available online too from certain companies that supply necessities.

Jay

If this is possible, it's a mistake for businesses.

It's probably called a "personal assistant." I want one of those to keep me stocked, run my errands, drive me around, pick up my kids, etc. Honestly though, if Fresh Direct has a feature like this, maybe it makes sense for a department store, too.

replenishment system for makeup, hosiery, etc. Is this possible?

Liz

That could work nicely for some, but not for me.

Would I like a driver? Yes. A cook? Yes. Someone to remind me to sleep? Yes. But replenish my underwear? No, thanks. Shopping is like dessert for me—there is always room.

Craig

Specialty stores look for ways to accommodate their customers and offer a better service— ask and you shall receive.

If they do not accommodate you, I would look to another retailer.

Travel

"I travel light. I think the most important thing is to be in a good mood and enjoy life, wherever you are."

—Diane von Furstenberg

71

What do you think are the most important items to

Joyce

The must-have basics.

Lingerie, night gowns, slippers, warm up suit (to hang out in the room or maybe go to the gym), umbrella, and depending where and what the trip is for—two pairs of slacks, 3–4 tops, shawl, coat of some kind, makeup, phone charger, and a small travel steamer.

Nancy

For a city vacation, I pack black basics in lightweight wool or silk.

A few pairs of pants. Jeans. A skirt. A dress or two. A leather jacket. Light sweaters or tees. Shawls. Jewelry to mix it up. Walking shoes and "going out for cocktails" shoes. Beauty products. For the beach, the same idea applies, but I lighten the colors and add shorts, bathing suits, flip flops, and a straw hat.

Jay

Depending on the season—one pair of sensational shoes for everything.

If they are slightly "uncomfortable" then buy insoles. Stop complaining and look chic. For women—one everyday with everything shoe and one heel if possible. If not, a chic flat with insole for all. A perfect flat can give an evening look instant Japanese appeal. One perfect coat or jacket. Get something in a perfect fabric and solid color that may or may not have weather protective properties. Two pairs of pants and one perfect white shirt or blouse. Change the

take on every trip?

ways you wear it and bring extra accessories (belts, jewels, etc). For me, I always wear the shoe and jacket I want for the whole trip. I pack two sweaters, two pants, and two shirts (one white, one blue). *Always.* I might pack a pair of pajamas and extra socks and underwear. Tons of magazines! I subscribe to everything and have no time to read any of them. Traveling to me is magazine time!

Liz

A short list.

Shoes. Socks. Underwear. Tops that work for day/night; casual pants and a dress and/or skirt. Toothbrush, face wash, q-tips.

Craig

Basics work.

Based on your travel agenda, you should always consider a basic day to evening dress, jacket and pant where each/all can be accessorized accordingly. Fill in with knits, because they take little room, coordinate with your outfits, and don't wrinkle. As travel becomes more restrictive, consider single color palettes where all pieces can be worn together and separately to make your day to evening looks easy and elegant.

72

Do you have any tips on folding different clothing when using

Pack the heaviest things on the bottom of the case.

Joyce
Try to make the least amount of folds per item. For instance, fold only the sleeves of a jacket in and only fold from the bottom to the top of the jacket. Spread things out as flat as you can.

Roll.

Nancy
Roll, not fold.

No.

Jay
No tips from me.

a suitcase?

Roll.

Liz

You can iron/steam it first, then roll it. This works well for anything without embellishment and saves a lot of room.

On a roll.

Craig

To avoid wrinkles, roll your clothes when possible and add tissue paper and/or dry cleaning plastic around the natural fibers, i.e., silks, wools, cottons and rayon that tend to wrinkle more easily.

73

Do you believe in packing ahead of time or just before a trip?

Joyce

I try to pack a few days ahead of a trip.

I hate leaving something home that I feel I need on a trip. I start with putting in my lingerie, slippers, nightgown, and then proceed with the clothing items and shoes. Lastly, I decide on jewelry and accessories.

Nancy

When it comes to clothing, I am unable to plan ahead.

I marvel at those who plan their whole week's attire over the previous weekend. Because I dress according to my mood at the moment, I find it impossible to pack well in advance of leaving for a trip or in advance of beginning my work week. I wish I could. I am sure there are wonderful advantages to planning and packing ahead. It would be far less frantic and I could leave the house in a peaceful mood and arrive at the airport on time!

Jay

Depends.

I pack the night before with wine. It helps me do first and think later. If I had an event or something very specific I was traveling to, I would definitely plan in advance to make sure my needs were met. Otherwise, just pack the night before.

What are the advantages?

Liz

Packing just before a trip may prevent overpacking.

Always just before unless you need very specific things that you may have to buy. If you need the perfect gown or dress for a big event then sure plan it out. Packing just before helps me pack light. I guess it depends on your personality as well. I would never, ever forget something, but I would definitely overpack. Last minute packing encourages me to make practical decisions. Also, people take new outfits or think they will put together new outfits when on a trip but who actually ends up having time to do that? You should take your favorite items that you can rely on and just throw and go.

Craig

Plan ahead.

What are the advantages? Pack ahead of time and reduce your stress! Make a list and stick to your list to avoid over packing. If you travel a lot, keep basics together to avoid a lot of work when planning.

Do you pack things on hangers or in plastic? How?

Joyce

I often pack things on wire hangers in plastic dry cleaner bags.

Wire hangers don't take up take up too much room and I can leave them at the hotel. I find this really helps eliminate wrinkles. I always pack a portable steamer too, just in case.

Nancy

Sometimes, if weight and space allows, I keep my clothing on the wire hangers from the drycleaner.

Every piece is on a hanger in an individual plastic bag. I rotate; that is, half of the garments' hangers are at the top of the suitcase, and the other hangers are at the bottom of the suitcase. It's easy to unpack and hang, and the garments travel almost wrinkle-free. Even wire hangers add extra weight though, and now that weight restrictions are strict, I am less likely to travel with them.

Jay

Folding is best.

I fold mostly, but the roll idea seems to be popular. Wrinkles don't bother me. I like something to look a little lived in as it makes the fabric seem more alive. If it's something you don't want wrinkled, I would wear it so I don't smash it in a suitcase or I would bring things in fabrics that don't get so wrinkled. If you're worried about wrinkles, I would just hang the stuff up in a bathroom and turn on the hottest water from the shower to steam.

I am trying to avoid unnecessary wrinkles.

No hangers.

Liz
Roll in plastic.

Use plastic always.

Craig
Avoid hangers unless you are staying somewhere they may not be available. Use plastic as it prevents many wrinkles, protects your clothes, and actually helps keep the interior space of your case more flexible so everything will fit easier.

75

Can you help me edit my selections for a trip?

Joyce

Build around one neutral color.

I decide on one basic color and build my travel wardrobe around it. In the winter, it is usually black; in the summer, it is a lighter color with black added too. I will often take complete outfits, for instance, a pantsuit or a skirt-suit. Though the trend today is not to match clothing so much, I find in traveling this is the easiest for me. I take a flat shoe and a heel. I carry a larger hand bag and take a smaller one for evening. I add a cardigan, several tops and accessories. I always take a jacket or raincoat and umbrella. Often, I pack earlier in the week. Sometimes, I go back and take out a few items. I never take more than one suitcase. If I cannot get it in one suitcase, I leave it at home.

Nancy

The simple answer is to pack all of your basic pieces in one neutral color.

If I were going on a trip to an urban location, for instance, I am pretty sure I could survive with these pieces in my favorite neutral (black): a great jacket (maybe leather, depending on the weather), one pair of casual trousers (maybe jeans) and one pair of dressier trousers, one skirt, and maybe a dress. For tops: a cashmere sweater, a tank top, and some tees. I would add interest with accessories. If the skirt, trousers and dress could be knitted—even better. I try to expand each item's use; for instance, I have a small black Louis Vuitton Epi cosmetic case that I use for an evening bag.

I always seem to pack too much.

Pack light.

Jay

Remember that you will have to carry your suitcase with you. Don't bother worrying and PACK LIGHT. Be chic. Less is more in this case and you don't need a million things when you go away. One can never seem to pack the right pieces anyway. Just be decisive and live with it. Blame the wine I suggested while packing!

Last minute packing.

Liz

Again, packing at the last minute helps. I usually pick out two bottoms (pants, shorts, skirt) then match a few tops instead of the other way around because you probably have more tops than bottoms—this helps eliminate items. You shouldn't have to wear a whole new ensemble everyday so take a pair of pants you can wear with several tops. Also, pick your shoes earlier rather than later so you don't end up taking all of them. Be realistic about weather and what you will be doing but don't over-prepare. Also, remember you might buy something; this always encourages me to leave plenty of room.

Plan ahead.

Craig

Planning and packing ahead is the easiest way to avoid over-packing. Use pieces that coordinate in one or two color palettes. If in doubt, do without!

76

What basic accessories would you include?

Joyce

A few items.

A shawl, a scarf(s), belt, jewelry (often very simple jewelry to travel—all gold or all silver with some pearls), and an extra, smaller handbag.

Nancy

Jewelry and more.

With garment choices as minimal as I described before, I would not keep accessories basic. I would choose large, important jewelry pieces with the power to transform a look. I still like pashmina scarves and treasure an over-sized cashmere wrap that also serves as a blanket on the flight.

Jay

Edit your selections.

A perfect cashmere blanket that you wrap around yourself for evening and cozy up to on a plane, train, or car. Sparkling water. Perfect shoes as I said before—one chic everything shoe and one chic "evening" pair. Jewels, if you want them.

A short list.

Liz

A comfortable pair of shoes that works with everything and an amazing pair for special times. A big bag for traveling and a smaller one for night. One belt, to be safe. A needle and thread for buttons and hems. A statement ring and necklace.

Four categories.

Craig

One or two large scarves or wraps, some basic jewelry, two pairs of shoes, and a large and small handbag.

77

How do you limit your shoe choices? I seem to take too many shoes.

Joyce

Choose one color.

By selecting one basic color for your clothing, you are better able to take fewer shoes. I usually travel in a flat shoe. I take one or two medium heels and if I plan to go to a gym, my work out shoes.

Nancy

Three pairs in one color will do.

We run into trouble with shoes for two reasons: **1.** The lack of really comfortable choices; and **2.** A refusal to limit our wardrobes to one neutral color. Shoes can be kept to a maximum of three pairs: a flat, a heel, and perhaps an evening shoe. A ballet flat or a driving shoe works well for travel days since you don't have to untie them in the security line. I also pack flip-flops instead of slippers.

Jay

Be strict with yourself.

Just say: I'm bringing two pairs. If you're doing something beachy, bring a sandal. Done.

Liz

Start with the shoes.

Select two to three pairs for a week of travel. Then, create outfits around them. Shoes take up too much space to over pack them. Also wear the biggest and heaviest ones on the plane, and no that pair doesn't have to count toward the two to three.

Craig

Three pairs will do.

Two pairs to fill the basic plan—one walking/ daytime shoe and one evening shoe. Anything more is a luxury, so consider your space! Shoes take a lot of room. You should always keep a pair of flip-flops stashed to wear in the hotel room.

78

Which fabrics travel best?

"Which fabric travels
worst?" would be a
better question.

Joyce

I think those would include linen, and any
item containing linen, silk, and cotton. I like
gabardine, wool, some polyester blends. I
usually take a small steamer so this does not
really concern me.

Nancy

Three.

Lightweight wools, silk, and knits.

Jay

Many different
fabrications.

I travel with cotton shirts, linen shirts (wrinkles
make me happy), all different fabrications in
pants. Cashmere sweaters… I don't know. I
travel in what feels good to me and take the
occasion as a time to dress nicely. NEVER A
TRACK SUIT. Disgusting.

Wool and cotton.

Keep it simple.

Liz
Anything thicker obviously holds up better than lightweight fabrics

Craig
Synthetics such as polyester and polyamide may not be your fabric of choice to wear daily, but they are easy travel clothes. Silks and wools will wrinkle but hang and steam out easily. Consider knits a mainstay for travel!

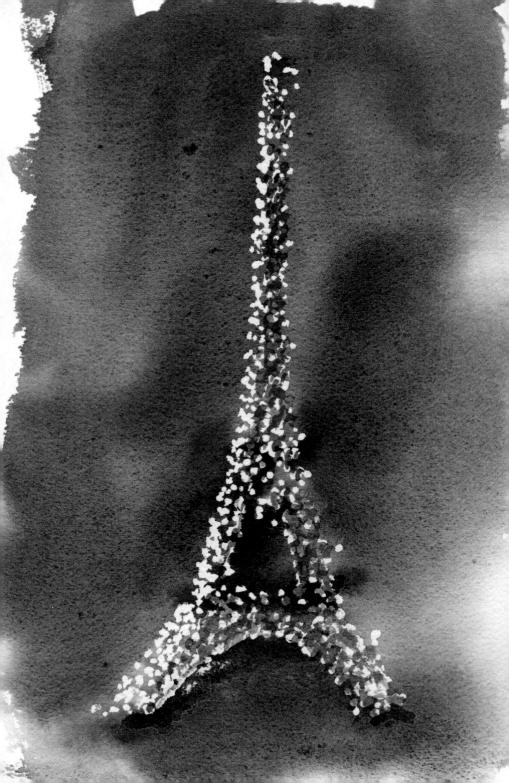

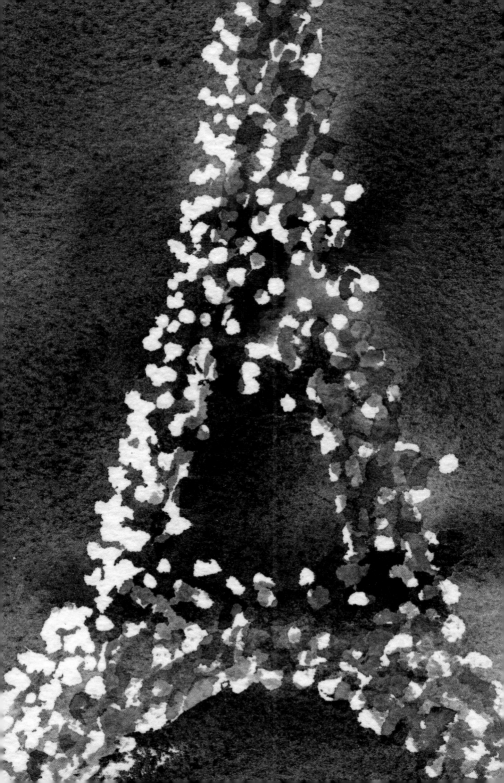

79

What do you suggest taking in a carry-on?

Joyce

Items that calm my nerves.

I am not the best flyer so I take a lot of magazines, chewing gum, phone charger, medicines, and a plastic bag that the airport requires with my makeup, camera, and my trip schedule.

Nancy

It depends on whether the trip is a long or short one.

Mine is unwisely always packed with books. I now love the Kindle or the iPad. After having both a camera and a bag of jewelry stolen from packed luggage, I always pack these valuables in my carry-on. Then, certain toiletries that I use to refresh en route. For long travel, I pack a lightweight cashmere wrap, head rest, etc. For shorter travel, a lightweight wrap or sweater to protect against the weird inconsistencies in airplane temperatures.

Jay

Everything in my carry on.

I NEVER check a bag. I bring everything in a leather duffle so that I can keep it easy and light. Literally never check anything.

Liz

Duffle bags.

The only time I do carry-on is if I can use a duffle. Get one with wheels if you need to, but when I think carry-on, I think collapsible.

Craig

Necessities only.

Anything you may need if stranded in the airport for hours! Cell phone charger, book, energy bar, hand wipes, and if you can fit a day's change of clothes, do it!

80

What are some non-clothing items to include in your suitcase

Joyce

Zipbags are a must. As are a small steamer, an umbrella, and my name and phone number somewhere in the suitcase in case it gets lost. I use plastic zip sweater bags to pack my lingerie and hosiery. In another plastic zip bag, I put my night gown and slippers. I once had to open my suitcase. As inspectors went through it, everything fell all over the floor. I was quite embarrassed. Now, I try to have everything in these zip sweater bags and they just scan them.

Nancy

Again, books. Thank goodness for the recent addition of e-books—removes 10 pounds from the suit-case! Then, I pack other electronics (iPod, hair styling tools, adaptor, converter, etc.), accessories, toiletries, and medication. I also travel with a small manicure kit, a tiny sewing kit, and travel-sized make-up brushes.

when you travel?

Jay

Necessities. Alcohol, sparkling water, and a *Teen Vogue*. That will get you through everything!

Liz

A short list. Toothbrush, comb, face wash, body-butter, a nail file, a sketchbook/notebook, pens, and candy.

Craig

Don't forget: Small candle, Febreeze wrinkle release spray, energy bars, and an MP3 player.

The Ultimate:
If You Could
Have Just One...

"I'm nothing to look at, so the only thing
I can do is dress better than anyone else."
—Wallis Simpson

81

If you could have but one jacket?

Joyce

Chanel. Classic, chic, and timeless.

Nancy

Rick Owens. Black leather.

Jay

Men: *Jil Sander* double face. The proportion is current but still feels traditional and timeless. The designers are so genius! Maybe a collage jacket from *Comme des Garcons*—I wanted one that mixed gingham with navy wool. When I went back to try it on, it was gone! Women: *Marni.* I think it's proportionally interesting and I think they pay close attention to their fabrics and the combination of tech versus familiar. Something in washed wool from *Yohji*—amazing.

Liz

Jil Sander or *Calvin Klein* both are wearable, beautiful and have an understated modern twist. *Rick Owens,* of course, for something edgy and divine.

Craig

A *Craig Signer*—My Modern Model #1—an updated fit with a zip or button-front fly collar that can be worn day or evening and is a core wardrobe element.

82

Black trousers?

Joyce
Max Mara. The fit is great.

Nancy
Balenciaga. But if not, I love a wide-legged, high-waisted silhouette. I hate linings.

Jay
Men: I love a natural waistline and slim leg with a long crotch. Also I love a natural waistline with a pleated, wide leg, and long crotch. I believe in the long crotch either way to change the silhouette for men! Women: *Jil Sander* tailored pants. *Donna Karan* stretch pant from 7 easy pieces.

Liz

Jil Sander is an expert! *The Row* has the most flattering leggings I have ever seen. *Ralph Lauren* always comes out with something classic in a new and interesting fabric. *Phi* offers a sexier version of the classic black pant.

Craig

My *Craig Signer* Social #1—gorgeous Italian silk pant with a luscious feel that can coordinate with any top or jacket in lieu of a dress for any occasion.

83

Pair of shoes?

Joyce

Chanel. Up-to-date and wearable.

Nancy

My perfect shoe is a black heel with an ankle strap. It is beautiful soft leather and when the heel gets caught in a grate or rubbed against the back of a stair, the leather does not crunch up. It is an imaginary shoe and is very comfortable. The maker of my imaginary shoe is not really important, but I wouldn't mind if it were *Dior.* I also would love to have a pair of *Lanvin* ballet flats and a pair of boots by *Hermès.* On the simple side, I like *Havaianas* flip flops and *Puma* sneakers.

Jay

Men: *Jil Sander*—heavy and masculine, but with a nod to a streamlined shape, old school cobbler detailing, and minimal seam interest. If not Jil, then *Dries van Noten.* They have the chicest men's shoes. They don't look affected yet they still pull off the vibe of fashion due to the creator's sensitivity to shape, material, and fabric combinations. Women: *Vivienne Westwood*—she treats shoes like the dresses she drapes. They are so chic, fabric/skin oriented, and always have the sensibility to not take themselves too seriously. *Prada*—they have the best heel shapes every season. I am always in love with their shoes!

Liz

Prada always has the most interesting styles, definitely worth the investment but will probably always be recognizable as the shoe for that year. If you want something a little more subtle but forward, I'd go with *Miu Miu* as they just take it down a notch. *Jeffrey Campbell* always offers an amazing on-trend selection of shoes at a great value for girls who have to talk the talk but still like to walk the walk as well.

Craig

Christian Louboutin's classic heel in neutral.

84

Earring?

Joyce
2.5 carat diamond studs work with everything.

Nancy
The perfect pair would be a big, platinum hoop.

Jay
Jil Sander Calder-inspired. *Darcy Miro* has change-your-life metal pieces. *Alexander Calder* jewelry! Anything large and important. I feel that sometimes the important, strange material, oddly shaped things are the "go with everything" piece—a *Ted Muehling* maybe. Something turquoise, too.

Liz
I haven't worn earrings since I lost my pair of *Venetian* glass cubes, but I am working towards owning a pair from *Darcy Miro*'s collection. I think earrings are fun, but for the most part, unnecessary objects.

Craig
Diamond studs large enough to be noticed, but not so large to distract.

85 Handbag?

Joyce
Bottega Veneta tote bag in a neutral color.

Nancy
Dior.

Jay
Bottega leather in a larger shape. *Henry Beguelin* abstract shapes. Vintage crocodile *Hermès.*

Liz
Prada. Vintage beaded and embroidered bags for evening.

Craig
Hermès Birkin.

86

Watch?

Joyce
Cartier tank.

Nancy
Cartier tank.

Jay
Something vintage and handsome.

Liz
Vintage thin. I want 20 of them on one arm.

Craig
Franck Muller—adding fun to wildly beautiful timepieces.

87 Coat?

Joyce
Long, black *Armani.*

Nancy
The Row sand colored cashmere and ermine.
To die for.

Jay
Men: Something unconstructed, soft, and life
changing; *Armani* without all the "stuff" on it.
Women: *Lanvin*—chic fabric, bias cut wool,
all about the fabric and shape. So genius and
wears like a sweater. Not pretentious and has
the ability to go stylish and polished or easy
and nothingness! Love!

Liz
Still *Jil Sander* and *Calvin Klein.*

Craig
Sable.

88

Raincoat?

Joyce
Burberry trench coat with removable lining.

Nancy
Black dolman sleeved voluminous and hooded—beautiful for day and evening.

Jay
Something by a designer who is smart enough not to call their style a "raincoat," but has all the properties of a raincoat and that wicks away the water. I love advanced fabric technology.

Liz
Not sure, have been looking for one for a year.

Craig
A classic black trench that can be worn anywhere at anytime—**Burberry.**

89

Necklace?

Joyce
Gold, solid, thick chain, 14 inches long.

Nancy
Huge, huge opera-length pearls.

Jay
Something huge and imposing in any material or no necklace at all—anything middle bores me.

Liz
Big—simple or insanely detailed, as long as it's big, otherwise the neck is beautiful and elegant on its own.

Craig
Pearls. Strands and strands of pearls mixed with diamonds, and more pearls.

90 Belt?

Joyce
Black alligator, 2.5 inches wide.

Nancy
Chanel with lots and lots of chains and pearls and whatever!!

Jay
Women: *Elsa Peretti* ivory (actual tusk) hardware with a crocodile strap. My friend has this on a leather strap and it's so amazing!!! On the more exotic strap, the better.

Liz
Vintage. What's the point if it's not unique and doesn't add something to or change your silhouette? Your clothes should fit without one.

Craig
Hermès.

"Vintage. What's the point if it's not unique and doesn't add something to or change your silhouette?"

The Critics

Mary Baskett,
Mary Baskett Gallery

This new fashion book is a must read for all who want to know what really happens in the great world of clothes and runways. It gives you practical tips to look your best and to defend yourself against detractors. There are so many ways to answer a question. I loved it.

Victoria Morgan,
Artistic Director and CEO, Cincinnati Ballet

When I read though sections of *Collective Fashion Wisdom,* I realized that since my on-stage days as a professional dancer, where I was clothed by long-standing designers who were not only highly experienced, but dedicated to capturing the essence of the communication in a piece of choreography, I have been more instinctual and random about my sense of fashion. The thing that is really great about this book is that it gives the reader very concrete, useable ideas about how to capture your essence and expression through the clothes you wear in a strategic, organized, definable, and budgetary manner. For me, this book helped to bring order to the chaos that is called my walk-in closet. Posture, line, energy, placement in space, coloration, texture, attitude, flow, and rhythm can all wreak havoc if simply placed together in a big bowl and spun around. But havoc can dissolve into order, class, power, and a unified expression when combined in ways that compliment and more deeply finesse your outward communication. If you are interested in becoming more of who you want to be, better read *Collective Fashion Wisdom!*

David Meister,
Fashion Designer

A great read! It takes you for a fun run through the ups and downs and the ins and outs of fashion tips and style secrets. Sit back, have a cocktail and enjoy a fun read from some of Cincinnati's fashion best. Then, hit your closets, hit the stores, and have some fun experimenting and expanding your own personal look!

Kelley Downing,
President and CEO,
Bartlett & Co.

Joyce Elkus has written a must-have fashion guide for the tasteful business woman who doesn't have time for fashion magazines. She cuts through the fads and glitz to show the reader how to dress for success on any occasion.

Phyllis Brown
Lerner, *Attorney*

Much more than what to wear—this book provides answers on what to buy, what to keep, when to wear, how to organize, wish list purchases, and how to get the most for your money. Each question is answered from insider fashionistas with styles ranging from elegant and classic to minimalist/accessorizer to provocative purist to fabric specialist to "idea fairy." There is a point of view—or a combination of them—that gives an answer to all of your fashion questions.